Stand Up Paddleboarding

by
Robert Stehlik

for
dummies®
A Wiley Brand

Stand Up Paddleboarding For Dummies®

Published by: **John Wiley & Sons, Inc.,** 111 River Street, Hoboken, NJ 07030-5774, www.wiley.com

For general information on our other products and services, please contact our Customer Care Department within the U.S. at 877-762-2974, outside the U.S. at 317-572-3993, or fax 317-572-4002. For technical support, please visit https://hub.wiley.com/community/support/dummies.

Wiley publishes in a variety of print and electronic formats and by print-on-demand. Some material included with standard print versions of this book may not be included in e-books or in print-on-demand. If this book refers to media such as a CD or DVD that is not included in the version you purchased, you may download this material at http://booksupport.wiley.com. For more information about Wiley products, visit www.wiley.com.

Library of Congress Control Number is available from the publisher.

ISBN: 978-1-394-27629-5 (pbk); 978-1-394-27630-1 (ebk); 978-1-394-27631-8 (ebk)

SKY10099063_022625

Contents at a Glance

Table of Contents

CHAPTER 4: **Paddle Perfection: Finding a Match to Propel You Forward** 43

CHAPTER 5: **Safety Dance: Take a Chance, but Don't Leave the World Behind** 51

CHAPTER 6: **Shielding Yourself from the Elements** 63

CHAPTER 7: **Preparing for the Big Blue** 71

Introduction

Confucius is credited with having said, "Our greatest glory is not in never falling but in rising every time we fall." This ode to perseverance and resilience applies especially well to stand up paddleboarding (SUP), where any progress you make is usually accompanied by many falls. Everyone takes a dunking, especially when you're just starting out. Even as you progress in the sport — going out in more challenging conditions; using a smaller, tippier board; or trying out a new discipline or maneuver, for example — falling into the water is always part of the process. I may even argue that if you're never falling in, you aren't challenging yourself enough.

So, yes, SUP is a glorious metaphor for life itself. It's not about staying perfectly balanced and upright all the time. (No one does.) It's about laughing off wobbles and wipeouts and about getting back on the board with a smile, no matter how many times you get knocked off. That's where the glory comes in; as your balance and fitness improve, you can conquer new challenges. You realize that every time you fall and get back up you learn something and get a little better and stronger.

Maybe you've never tried to SUP but are curious. Maybe you're already an experienced paddler ready to take your skills to the next level or you want to teach others to enjoy this beautiful way to enjoy the water. If so, I wrote *Stand Up Paddleboarding For Dummies* for you. Welcome to the club!

About This Book

You may have heard that SUP is a great workout for your core muscles. That is true, but only if done right. Most beginners paddle using mostly their arms, cruising over calm water with little engagement of the rest of their body. In this book you will learn to paddle using not only your arms but to also engage the stronger muscles in your back, shoulders, legs, and yes, your core, using your whole body to propel yourself forward quickly and efficiently. Stand up paddling is perhaps the most enjoyable way to stay fit, both physically and mentally.

The sport looks quite easy when you're watching experienced paddlers from shore. They look balanced and calmly paddle at a steady pace, gliding over the water. After you try it, however, you realize that it's certainly not as easy as it looks; even seasoned paddlers keep finding ways to improve.

Stand Up Paddleboarding For Dummies is my effort to share the knowledge I've learned from other experts, through trial and error, and through teaching many people and seeing what they struggle with most — all in an easy-to-follow format. I've taught and coached thousands of people to SUP through lessons and free clinics, and watching beginners make the most common mistakes repeatedly has helped me refine the process of explaining the sport to make is as accessible as possible. In these pages, I show you how choose the right board for you, how to actually stand up on the thing, and what other gear you need before you hit the water. I break down the basics of paddle technique (spoiler: don't just use your arms) and introduce you to a variety of SUP disciplines for both casual and competitive paddlers. Along the way, you can find plenty of opportunities to enjoy the broader SUP lifestyle and community.

I can't say that writing this book was easy for me; it was one of the most challenging things I've done, and I sincerely hope not only that you enjoy it but also that it makes your life a little more fun.

Foolish Assumptions

I haven't made loads of assumptions about you as I've written this book, but I have assumed that at least some of the following may apply to you:

>> You're interested in finding out how to stand up paddleboard.

>> You tried SUP once or twice and struggled, but you aren't ready to give up yet.

>> You're upset because your partner was able to balance and you kept falling in.

>> You bought a SUP or received one as a gift but have no idea how to use it.

>> You've always been drawn to the water.

>> You've read some other *For Dummies* books and like the easy-to-follow format.

>> You were introduced to the sport, and now you're hooked.

>> You're already a seasoned paddler and want a reference book that helps you discover new ways to enjoy the sport.

How This Book Is Organized

Stand Up Paddleboarding For Dummies is divided into four sections with each part going into different aspects of the sport. Unlike a novel, you don't have to read it from cover to cover, each part is written to make sense on its own, so you can skip around and read what you are most interested in first and then get back to the other parts later. From learning about the history of the sport, understanding the equipment, preparing for getting your feet wet, to paddling for the first time, to progressing and trying different disciplines and enjoying the sport with others, my goal is to give you a complete overview that is easy to read and follow.

Part I: Before You Get Your Feet Wet

This section has a brief history of the sport and how it became one of the fastest growing sports in the world. I cover equipment knowledge and how to choose the right board and paddle for your needs. Part I also covers safety considerations and equipment, dressing for the occasion, and how to prepare for getting on the water.

Part II: Get Up, Stand Up

Armed with the knowledge and preparation from the first part, you are ready to get on the water! In this part you will learn the basics of carrying the board, launching safely, paddling on your knees, learn to steer the board, how to stand up, how to paddle in a straight line, turning around and getting back to shore safely. You will also learn about some of the most common beginner mistakes and how to avoid them.

Part III: Leveling Up: From Wobbly Novice to Zen Waterman

So, you're no longer a beginner and are ready for new challenges, in this part I go into mastering efficient stroke technique. As you get faster you can consider entering some SUP races and what's involved. If paddling in flat water is not exciting enough for you, you can also learn about catching some waves and SUP surfing technique, as well as doing downwinders and paddling in rough conditions.

Part IV: The SUP Lifestyle

SUP is more than a pastime, it's a lifestyle. In this part I get into the many health benefits of paddling and how to avoid injuries. You can enjoy the sport on your own but it's always fun to share the experience with others and many different ways to enjoy the sport socially. As SUP grows worldwide, there are efforts to make it an Olympic sport, which would broaden its appeal as a serious sport. I cover assessing damage, repairing your board and how to properly take care of your equipment. This part also has an adventure guide that will make you want to explore.

Part V: The Part of Tens

This part has lists of ten questions to ask yourself before buying a board, ten tips to go faster, ten ways to avoid injury, ten things you can do on a SUP, and ten resources to continue your quest to learn more with certifications, lessons, and other resources.

Icons Used in This Book

Every *For Dummies* book has some helpful icons pointing you in the direction of information that's sure to help you along your way. These are the icons I use in this book:

TIP

This icon marks simple pointers and nuggets that can make a big difference.

REMEMBER

I use the Remember icon to emphasize useful information — important points to remember for later use.

WARNING

You should always have a healthy respect for the water and for mother nature. This icon points out risks to avoid on and off the water.

TECHNICAL STUFF

When you see the Technical Stuff icon, you know that what you're about to read is interesting but ultimately not critical to understanding the topic at hand. If you're short on time or just want to get in and get out with the need-to-know info, you can skip these paragraphs.

Beyond the Book

In addition to the book text, which I consider a complete SUP manual, I've also created a Cheat Sheet that's a quick start guide to stand up paddleboarding. To get this resource, visit www.dummies.com and search for **stand up paddleboarding for dummies cheat sheet**.

Where to Go from Here

You can read this book from start to finish or bounce around depending on your needs. If you can't wait to get on the water, jump to Chapter 9. Before you buy a board, make sure to read

Chapters 3 and 19. You can also use the table of contents and index to find the topics that most interest you. I hope you do read the whole book eventually and get a lot of value from it. Thank you and enjoy!

1

Before You Get Your Feet Wet

Chapter **1**

What'SUP? Paddling While Standing up through History

S tand up paddleboarding (SUP) may seem to many like a modern invention, but the roots of this sport stretch far back to ancient civilizations. In its current form, SUP has only been around since the early 2000s, when Laird Hamilton and Dave Kalama picked up paddles during a 2004 photoshoot and realized how practical and fun standing and paddling on a big surfboard with a long paddle was. Since then, modern SUP has become a global phenomenon and undergone rapid growth.

I was fortunate enough to learn how to SUP back in 2007 from some of the early pioneers of the sport. Ever since, I've been passionate not only about participating in the sport myself but also about sharing the sport and stoke with others — which I hope to do in this chapter.

Paddling in a Standing Position: Ancient History

Humans have long been drawn to the water and paddling while standing up has been a natural evolution for many societies throughout history. So many early records of paddling while standing exist that it seems to be deeply rooted in human nature. In some places, the technique was born from necessity for fishing and transportation, while in others it became a cultural practice.

One of the earliest examples of standing up while paddling dates back as far as 3,000 years ago along the Peruvian coast, where fishermen used crafts called *caballitos de totora* (reed horses; see Figure 1-1) to navigate through the surf to fish in coastal waters. Paddlers could use a long paddle to steer these rafts, made from bundled reeds, from a kneeling or standing position. Paddling on the knees was more stable because of the lower center of gravity, but standing up on their reed crafts allowed the fishermen to stretch their legs, get a better view of the fish, and have more leverage on their paddles.

FIGURE 1-1: A *caballito de totora.*

LuisAlexanderMJ/Adobe Stock Photos

In Israel, a similar style of paddling emerged with the *hasake* — large, wide-bodied boats propelled by a standing rider with a long, two-sided paddle as shown in Figure 1-2. Early records of these crafts date back to the Roman Empire, and they're still being used in the Mediterranean Sea today (mostly by skilled lifeguards as a rescue tool, but also for fishing and recreation). In many ways, the *hasake* is a precursor to the modern stand up paddleboard; wide and stable, it's designed for utility and allows the paddler to stand up comfortably while navigating ocean waves and turbulent waters.

FIGURE 1-2:
A modern *hasake* off the Israeli coast.

Indigenous communities across the world have long engaged in stand up paddling. People in Polynesia, North America, Southeast Asia, Africa (see Figure 1-3), and New Zealand have all stood and paddled canoes and boats for a variety of reasons: fishing, transportation, navigation, and cultural ceremonies. These practices show that standing up while paddling has played an integral role in human survival and culture over millennia.

You can find countless other examples of paddling while standing up, including the gondoliers of Venice, loggers navigating rivers and rapids on wooden logs, and canoeists.

REMEMBER

Surveying the Rise of SUP Surfing in Hawaii

While Polynesian canoes were mostly paddled in a sitting position, it was not uncommon for ancient Polynesians to paddle standing up, allowing a better vantage point of the reef below, making it easier to spot fish, and to get a better view of the horizon, weather, and other things in the distance.

The modern version of stand up paddling on a big surfboard began to evolve in the early 20th century, specifically in Waikiki, Hawaii. When the first hotels opened there in the early 1900s, the local surfers began to make a living as surf instructors, lifeguards, and entertainers. These locals were known as *beach boys* and would paddle out on large surf boards and *outrigger canoes* (canoes with side float attachments) to introduce tourists to riding waves. Taking a canoe paddle on a surfboard allowed them to paddle faster as they gave lessons. Paddling on a large surfboard with a paddle became known as *beach boy surfing*; the Hawaiian name for it is *Hoe he'e nalu* (stand, paddle, surf a wave).

Allow me to introduce you to some of the main beach boy surfers of yesteryear:

>> Duke Kahanamoku was born in 1890 to parents from prominent Hawaiian *ohana* (families). He grew up in Waikiki, close to Queen's Beach, where his statue, shown in Figure 1-4, stands today. Duke spent much of his youth at the beach, where he developed his surfing and swimming skills. He was a powerful swimmer and started breaking world records at local swim meets. He went on to win the gold medal in the100-meter freestyle at the 1912 Stockholm Olympics, followed by several other Olympic medals. He is also credited with introducing surfing to Australia, during a visit in 1914, and later to California, where he performed as an actor in Hollywood.

Australian lifeguards that Duke trained gave him an early *surf ski,* a big wooden board with a long two-sided paddle, as a gift. Duke Kahanamoku paddled this board and caught waves standing up with the long paddle.

TIP

To find out more about Duke Kahanamoku's legacy, check out the 2021 documentary *Waterman*.

FIGURE 1-4: Duke Kahanamoku statue.

Torval Mork/Adobe Stock Photos

» In 1940, John "Zap" Zapotocky moved from Pennsylvania to Waikiki and was inspired by watching Duke Kahanamoku. He ordered a custom-made long wooden paddle and started using it with his large longboard to ride the waves in Waikiki. Zap went on to be one of the sport's most enduring figures, SUP surfing in Waikiki until he was in his 90s. He witnessed the sport becoming a global phenomenon before he passed away in 2013.

» Well-known Waikiki Beach Boy John "Pops" Ah Choy used a large wooden surfboard and long paddle to teach surfing and take photos of tourists. His sons Bobby and Leroy Ah Choy carry on the legacy and host an annual Pops Ah Choy Surf Fest in Waikiki.

Breaking down the Modern SUP Revolution: Blame Laird

The modern era of SUP surfing started at an Oxbow photoshoot on the south shore of Maui in 2004. Laird Hamilton and Dave Kalama were surfing on big longboards in offshore winds. They noticed that they could just stay standing up on their boards after catching a wave while the offshore breeze would carry them back out to the lineup. Dave decided to get a couple of canoe paddles from his car, and he and Laird had a blast using them while standing on the boards.

They immediately ordered longer paddles from Malama Chun, a local paddle maker, and started designing specialized boards for

SUP surfing. Their experimentation and the influence they had as well-known watermen sparked the creation of modern stand up paddleboarding. That's why surfers like to "Blame Laird" for the popularity of SUP surfing.

Kindling the SUP flame

As the popularity of the sport began to grow, it quickly caught the attention of the global water sports community. On Oahu, Brian Keaulana picked up the sport and introduced a beach boy surfing division to the Buffalo Big Board Surfing Classic at Makaha in 2003, making it the first official SUP contest. The competition spurred rapid development of the sport, and both equipment and technique evolved quickly.

Keaulana, Dave Parmenter, and Todd Bradley started a company called C4 Waterman that was dedicated to developing SUP-specific boards, paddles, and equipment. Paddlesurf Hawaii and C4 Waterman were the first SUP-specific production boards available, and my business, Blue Planet Surf, was the distributor. Early adopters provided strong demand — so strong that it was impossible to keep up with in the early days of the sport. We held SUP clinics to introduce people to the sport, and I was fortunate enough to learn it from the best.

SUP quickly grew beyond its surfing roots into new disciplines, such as cruising, touring, racing, and downwinding, which accelerated growth. In 2006, the 32-mile Molokai to Oahu (M2O) Paddleboard World Championships introduced a SUP division. (Kevin Horgan won that race in 7 hours and 23 minutes.)

By 2008, several brands started producing SUP boards, which were sold and promoted mostly through surf and water sports retailers. My friends Jeff Chang and Doug Locke opened the first SUP-specific retail store, Wet Feet Hawaii, and were soon followed by many SUP-focused retail stores opening up around the world.

That same year, Gerry Lopez and Rainbow Sandals organized the first Battle of the Paddle in Dana Point with an unprecedented $25,000 prize purse. Also unprecedented was the spectator-friendly configuration of the race, a format now called "technical SUP race" (also see Chapter 16). It had a beach start, took competitors in and out through the surf, around buoys, and running through a series of tight turns on the beach and back out again for multiple rounds. The maximum board length allowed was 12 feet 6 inches, which created a whole new category of SUP boards. The excitement created through these events further solidified the sport's place in the competitive paddling world.

Tracing the explosive growth of SUP

Early adopters of the "new" sport were often already water sports enthusiasts that were eager to try something new. Surfers — especially older surfers with stiff backs and shoulders who found it difficult to paddle in a prone position and then pop up quickly while catching a wave — felt like *groms* (young surfers) all over again. Windsurfers and kitesurfers discovered SUP as a great activity when the wind was light. Canoe and kayak paddlers crossed over into SUP racing and whitewater SUP as a novel way to paddle. The introduction of inflatable boards that are easy to transport and store also played an important role in the world-wide growth of the sport.

Catching the World Wide Wave

SUP was the first major water sport where almost all information was available online. Traditionally, water sports enthusiasts got their information from print-based material and glossy magazines. The World Wide Web accelerated the development of equipment, technique, and hype. The accessibility of the sport, both in terms of the ease of getting the latest information (anywhere with Internet) and where it could be done (anywhere with water), quickly spread it to a much wider audience and helped stand up paddleboarding become the world's fastest growing water sport.

Making lemonade out of lemons

In Hawaii, the rapid growth of SUP had plateaued by 2019, but then the COVID-19 pandemic unexpectedly caused a renewed boom in popularity. During the global shutdowns of 2020 and

2021, when people were unable to go to the gym, travel, or go out with friends, SUP emerged as a perfect socially distanced activity. It offered people a way to stay active while being out on the water. SUP participation and sales of SUP equipment boomed during this period as more and more people from all walks of life discovered the versatility and appeal of the sport.

REMEMBER

According to the Outdoor Industry Association (OIA), by 2021, the global SUP market was valued at $1.4 billion, with tens of millions of participants having taken up the sport around the world. In the United States alone, an estimated 3.5 million people participated in SUP annually. A compound annual growth rate (CAGR) of approximately 10 percent is projected for the next decade.

Looking to the future

SUP continues to grow as more ways of enjoying the sport emerge and draw in a more diverse group of paddlers, with more women and young paddlers taking up the sport each year.

The growth of SUP foiling (see Chapter 22) has further expanded SUP disciplines, led to increased innovation and specialization, revolutionized downwind racing, and drawn many new athletes to the sport. SUP rentals continue to grow in popularity, especially in beautiful destinations around the world.

As of this writing, SUP is set to become part of the Olympics. (For more on that topic, see Chapter 16.) When that happens, it will open the sport to increased youth participation with support from national sports associations and establish SUP as a serious athletic pursuit.

REMEMBER

Although I can't say for sure what's next for SUP, I do know that innovation will continue and that new trends will emerge to quickly be taken up by dedicated water athletes around the world ready to take the next step in the evolution of the sport.

IN THIS CHAPTER

» Understanding how a board's length, width, and thickness affect performance

» Making sense of volume and how it relates to rider weight

» Understanding the parts of a board

» Leaning about board shapes

Chapter 2

Choosing the Right Board for Your Adventure

The first time I stood on a SUP was back in 2007. Balancing on the board was more challenging than I expected. Luckily, I had some of the pioneers of the sport giving me pointers and once I found my "sea legs," I quickly got hooked on the sensation of gliding over the water in a standing position. Sharing the joys of this sport by helping others get started has been my passion ever since.

Yes, You'll Need a Board

First things first: Let's address the elephant in the room — you'll need a board. While this may seem obvious, the sheer variety of boards available can be overwhelming for beginners.

But fear not, I'm here to help you navigate the waters and find the right fit for your needs.

Your first question may be "Should I buy an inflatable or a hard board?" It's a great question, and I'm glad you're thinking ahead. But before you decide on what type of board to get, you need to get a handle on how dimensions and shape influence a board's performance, so you have a better understanding of what size and shape work best for your needs. Ideally, you should try a few different boards before making a buying decision and this chapter will help you make sense of the differences.

TIP

If you're just dying to know whether you should go inflatable or stick with the tried-and-true hard board, check out Chapter 3, where I explain the differences and cover the practicalities of buying a new or used board.

Looking at dimensions: Length, width, and thickness

The length, width, and thickness of a SUP board play a crucial role in its performance on the water.

>> **Length:** Longer boards offer more glide and tracking (making it easier to paddle straight) as well as more stability (making them ideal for beginners and casual paddlers). On the other hand, shorter boards are more maneuverable and responsive, making them better suited for riding waves and for more experienced paddlers.

TIP

Most boards have the length, width, thickness and volume printed on the bottom or on the rail of the board.

REMEMBER

>> **Width:** The width of the board is the most important dimension to consider for side-to-side stability. A wider board (over 32 inches is considered wide) is more stable, making balancing on it easier. Narrow boards are faster because you have less board to push through the water (some race boards can be as narrow as 22 inches!). But they're also more tippy and not recommended for beginners.

>> **Thickness:** The thickness of the board is an indication of how much volume (floatation) a board has. However, because thickness is measured only at the thickest point, that dimension isn't as useful as knowing the volume of the board, which I cover in the following section.

Measuring volume and seeing how it relates to body weight

Volume is an important consideration when choosing a SUP board. Higher volume boards are more buoyant and can support heavier riders. Lower volume boards are suited for lighter riders and are usually lighter and easier to transport and store.

REMEMBER

Volume is usually measured in *liters of displacement.* By definition, one liter of volume provides one kilogram (2.2 pounds) of floatation. That means a 100-liter board can float up to 100 kilograms (220 pounds). As a beginner, you want a board that can float at least twice your weight, so about half the board's volume is submerged to support the weight on it (your weight plus the weight of the equipment).

Having a board with more volume isn't a problem, but it doesn't necessarily translate into more stability because a thicker board raises the center of gravity. (Your feet are higher off the water surface.) Thick, high-volume boards can also be more susceptible to wind and *side chop* (small waves hitting your rails from the side). So, finding a volume that matches your body weight and skill level is important. A board that's too big for you can feel cumbersome and corky, while a board that doesn't have enough volume is challenging to balance on, doesn't glide as well, and is very sensitive to shifting weight.

TIP

A good starting point for beginners is a board with roughly 1 liter of volume for each pound of bodyweight, so a rider that weighs 180 pounds should look for a board that has roughly 180 liters of volume. Smaller, lower volume boards perform better when riding on a wave, which is why more advanced SUP surfers generally try to use the smallest board they can still comfortably catch a wave on. The simple chart in Figure 2-1 correlates volume with body weight and skill level and can help you determine the right board volume for you.

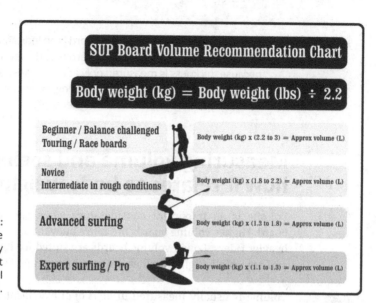

FIGURE 2-1:
Volume
chart by
bodyweight
and skill
level.

WARNING

You may be tempted to get a board that's too advanced for your skill level or too small for your body weight. Doing so will result in frustration and disappointment. Set yourself up for success by starting with a suitable board.

Listing the parts of a board

Before you dive into the specifics of board design, familiarize yourself with the names of its various components and how they influence performance. Figure 2-2 gives you the bird's eye view, and I look at each part in greater detail in the following bulleted list.

>> **Rails:** Paddleboarders call the sides of the board *rails*. Thicker, fuller rails add more volume to the sides of the board, which — as you may expect — makes the board more stable. Thinner rails don't provide the same amount of stability, but they *will* be more responsive in carving turns and less susceptible to side chop and wind.

Sharp edges on the rail (a rail variant referred to as *hard rails*) allow the water to *release* (instead of wrapping around the rail) when the board is *planing* (skimming over the water surface) at higher speeds. Rounded rails (called *soft rails*) are generally more forgiving and can reduce drag at lower speeds. Most all-around and SUP surfing boards have rails that transition from a fuller and softer rail shape in the front and middle to sharper and thinner rails toward the tail of the board. (See Figure 2-3.)

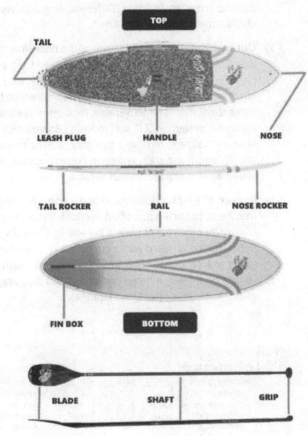

FIGURE 2-2: The parts of a board.

Rails

Full / boxy	Thin / tapered
Increased stability	Performance maneuverability
Increased glide	Decreased speed
Ideal for racing / touring	Ideal for surfing
Increased volume	Decreased volume
Not ideal for surfing	Not ideal for racing / touring

FIGURE 2-3: Rail shapes.

>> **Hull/bottom shape:** Most all-around and SUP surf boards have a *planing hull* (flat or slightly concave) that directs the water underneath the board to create lift and stability. Boards made for flat water touring or racing, however, often have *displacement hulls,* which are more rounded and direct the water around the hull to minimize drag at sub-planing speeds. You can read more about these options in the later section "Differentiating between displacement and planing hulls."

>> **Outline:** The *outline* is the shape of the nose (front), tail (back), and rails (edges) of the board viewed from above. (See Figure 2-4.) Boards with a narrow/pointy nose and tail have a more rounded outline in the middle, which tends to make them more maneuverable. (You often see that particular design on SUP surf models.) Boards with a wider nose and tail tend to have a straighter outline in the middle, which generally results in better tracking, glide, and speed while being less maneuverable.

>> **Rocker:** The *rocker* is the curve of the bottom of the board from nose to tail. People often overlook this particular feature, but the rocker plays a big role in a board's performance. A board with a curvy rocker is generally easier to turn and handles well in waves and rough water, while a board with a flatter rocker has less drag and more glide and tracks better (goes straight).

Tail

FIGURE 2-4:
Nose and
tail shapes.

Less surface area
Increased control
Less planing surface
Hollow / steep waves
Decreased speed
Tight turning arc

More surface area
Loose maneuverability
More planing surface
Small wave surfing
Increased speed
Wide turning arc

>> **Foil:** The differing thicknesses of the board from nose to tail. Most boards are thickest in the center where higher volume is needed to support the paddler in a standing position, and taper to thinner noses and tails, where less volume can be advantageous.

Inflatable boards are usually the same thickness from nose to tail. For more on that topic, check out Chapter 3.

>> **Deck:** Many SUPs have a flat *deck* (the top of the board) in the standing area simply because they're so much more comfortable to stand on than on the domed decks you often see on surfboard shapes. Some race boards have recessed decks that lower the center of gravity. I don't recommend recessed decks for beginners because those decks make getting back up on the board difficult.

>> **Deck pad:** The *pad* provides traction in the standing area. It also gives you padding and protects your feet and knees from the hard surface of the board.

>> **Handle:** Located in the center of weight of the board, the *handle* should allow you to carry the board without it being nose- or tail-heavy (with fins and leash attached to the board). The handle is recessed on the board's deck and should allow a comfortable, safe grip, ideally letting your fingers wrap around the handle.

>> **Vent plug:** Most boards have a *vent plug* to equalize pressure changes in the board resulting from temperature or altitude changes. Most vent plugs have a membrane that allows air to pass through but keeps water out. These self-venting plugs allow the board to automatically "breathe" and don't need to be removed manually.

>> **Leash and leash plug:** The *leash* is a cord connecting you to the board. You use the *leash plug,* located on the tail of the board to attach the leash to the board.

The leash is and always will be your most important piece of safety equipment.

>> **Fin:** The fin (also known as skeg) is mounted on the bottom/tail end of the board to keep it going straight, acting as a rudder in the water.

>> **Attachment points:** Some boards have additional attachment points for tie downs, cameras, and other equipment.

Considering Some Bells and Whistles

As in most things in life, you can get the plain vanilla version or the souped-up version. That means if plain vanilla is not your thing, you can add any number of additional features or accessories in order to enhance your SUP experience, including extended deck pads for SUP Yoga or paddling with pets, storage systems and attachment points for your paddle, equipment, dry bags, fishing rods, or camera mounts to get footage of your adventure. Colors and graphics are also important considerations for most buyers.

REMEMBER

There's a lot to choose from when it comes to tricking out your board, but keep in mind that, while these extras can be nice to have, the most important thing is finding a board size and shape that suits your needs and paddling style.

Thinking of fins and things (and shoes — and ships — and sealing-wax — of cabbages — and kings)

The fin in the back of the board is what allows the board to track well (go straight). In addition to that rudimentary task, fin design can noticeably affect how a board handles.

>> Bigger fins with more surface area usually improve tracking, and longer fins tend to make a board feel more stable. But ah, curses! More fin area also adds drag.

>> Side fins add more control in carving turns, and smaller fins let you turn the board more easily. Shorter boards made for SUP surfing usually have two or four side fin boxes in addition to a center fin box that allow you to install two or four side fins and a center fin. This arrangement allows you to use three or four fin setups for surfing (known as *2+1* and *quad fins,* respectively). The side fins provide extra hold in rail-to-rail carving turns while the board is planing on a wave. Longer boards usually need a center fin only; side fins have little benefit on these boards and add unnecessary drag.

Figure 2-5 shows you some possible fin arrangements.

Pondering the different shape and design philosophies

SUP board design is a blend of art and science. Board designers first visualize how a board's shape is going to interact with the water, and then they experiment with different versions of their ideas to come up with a shape that performs well for the intended use. Different shapes cater to various styles of paddling.

Board design is always a compromise, so don't expect one board to do everything perfectly. The challenge is to find a shape that's optimized for your weight, skill level, personal preference, and intended use.

REMEMBER

Differentiating between displacement and planing hulls

As I note earlier in the chapter, SUP hulls come in displacement and planing versions, which you can see in Figure 2-6.

SUP race boards and touring boards are usually displacement hulls designed to split the water with a pointy nose, have the water move around the hull, and then come back together by the tail of the board, creating minimal disturbance or drag.

Think of a sailboat shape with a pointy bow and a rounded, curvy hull. This type of shape aims to minimize drag at lower speeds and is faster in flat water conditions. Displacement hulls are usually pointy in the nose and have rounded rails, but the bottom under the standing area is still relatively flat because a fully rounded bottom would be very difficult to balance on.

TIP

All-around boards and SUP surf boards are usually planing hulls designed to create dynamic lift from water moving underneath the board (rather than around it as on a displacement shape). The bottoms of planing boards are flat or slightly concave and direct the water underneath the board to create lift. The rails on planing hulls usually have sharper edges toward the tail that allow the water to release (see Figure 2-7) when the board starts *planing*, or skimming, over the water surface at higher speeds (rather than wrapping round a curved rail). As the speed increases, you need less *wetted surface* (the amount of board surface in contact with the water) to create lift, which in turn reduces drag.

FIGURE 2-6:
Displacement hull race boards (left) and a SUP surfing board with planing hull (right)

MarekPhotoDesign.com/Adobe Stock Photos   *ohrim/Adobe Stock Photos*

FIGURE 2-7:
A SUP surfer planes over the water surface; water releases off the sharp rails.

Board is "planing" and water is "releasing" off the sharp rails

A planing hull usually has more drag than a displacement hull at low speeds, but after it starts planing, drag greatly reduces, and you can reach higher speeds by moving your weight farther back on the board so that less and less of the board is touching the water. Once you're planing, you can also steer these boards by leaning into a turn.

REMEMBER

Whether you're cruising on flat water, riding waves, or racing across the open ocean, you can find a hull shape designed to optimize performance and make the most out of your time on the water.

Chapter **3**

Shopping for SUP Gear

Welcome to Chapter 3 of *Stand Up Paddleboarding For Dummies!* If you've made your way through Chapters 1 and 2, you likely have a handle on the basics of board dimensions and shapes. (If you haven't checked those chapters out, you may want to do so before you buy a board.) In this chapter, you get a chance to explore the wide array of board options available to paddlers, from different construction options to specialized designs for different types of paddling adventures.

As a board designer and retail store owner, I love hearing from customers that SUP has improved their quality of life. In terms of your physical and mental health, this sport can be truly life changing. That's why my staff and I are passionate about helping customers find the perfect board to enjoy this journey. In this chapter, I pass on our collective wisdom about what to look for when shopping for a board.

So Many Choices: Breaking down the Board Bonanza

After you've tried a few different boards on your own and have realized how much fun you can have while getting the physical and mental benefits of standup paddleboarding, you'll want to get your own gear.

TIP

My advice? Don't break the bank on your first board; get a good beginner board — something that fits your current needs.

Getting a board that feels a bit tippy and challenging at first is also okay because your balance will improve quickly. But don't go overboard (pun intended) in the opposite direction either. I often see customers who overestimate their ability and buy a board that's too advanced for their skill level. This situation often leads to getting frustrated, going on the water less, or even completely giving up on this amazing sport. Don't be that person!

REMEMBER

Keep it simple. The goal is to have fun and enjoy!

Comparing inflatable and hard boards

In this section, I look at the pros and cons of inflatables versus hard boards so you can make an informed decision.

TIP

You always encounter a trade-off between portability and performance. Ideally, you should try both an inflatable and a hard board before buying a board so you can feel the difference for yourself. If you're a beginner planning to cruise on calm water, an inflatable will probably work well as a starter board. If you want better performance, especially to ride waves or to paddle in rougher conditions, consider a hard board. A majority of beginners purchase iSUPs, as they are convenient and relatively inexpensive, which has facilitated the continued growth of the sport.

Inflatable boards (iSUPs)

Here are some of the advantages and disadvantages of an inflatable board.

» Pros

- Less likely to get dinged (bounces off rocks)
- Usually more affordable
- Safe (softer surface)
- Portable; easy to ship, store, and transport

» Cons

- Less rigid than hardboards; can bend under feet and feel less stable, especially for heavier paddlers
- Same thickness and rail shape from nose to tail
- Thick nose and tail are sensitive to wind and choppy water
- Requires more time to inflate and deflate
- Materials and glue can deteriorate over time; sensitive to heat and UV damage (not recommended for tropical climates)
- Can puncture from sharp objects; difficult to repair leaking seams

Hard boards

Hard boards have their own set of benefits and downfalls.

» Pros

- Better performance (rail shape, volume distribution, and foil can be optimized; flip to Chapter 2 for more on the rail and foil board parts)
- Stiff; more responsive; can feel more stable and experience less drag
- Long life expectancy if properly maintained
- Often lighter weight

» Cons

- Less convenient for storage and transportation

- Needs to be handled more carefully; more likely to get dinged

- Higher initial cost

Seeing why board weight and construction matter

Heavy boards can have some advantages in certain conditions (namely strong winds or rough conditions where the weight and momentum of a heavier board are more stable and easier to control). In most cases, though, a lighter-weight board is preferable. Lighter boards are easier to carry, are more responsive, and accelerate with less effort. They also accelerate more quickly and have less swing weight (the weight at the front of the board that has to be moved from side to side to turn the board), which makes them feel livelier and easier to maneuver.

Although manufacturers can easily make a board lighter by using less material, doing so also makes it more fragile. A fragile board dings or cracks easily and can take on water. The last thing you want is a board that gets damaged easily. Ideally you want a board with a good weight-to-strength ratio that combines a relatively light weight with good strength and durability.

REMEMBER

Making cheap boards that are strong (but heavy) by adding more material is possible. But making a board that's both lightweight and strong takes special manufacturing techniques and premium materials that are generally more labor intensive and expensive. I cover some of the many construction options available for both inflatable and hard boards in the following sections.

TIP

Although most SUPs look similar and the differences in construction and quality aren't always obvious, you get what you pay for. Many cheap boards you can order online are low quality and may fail quickly. Whether you're shopping for an inflatable or hard board, buying from a reputable brand that offers at least a one-year warranty and quality accessories can save you money in the long run.

Looking at inflatable board construction

For many first-time buyers, an inflatable board seems like the ideal choice — it's inexpensive and easy to store, transport, and order online.

Inflatable SUPs (iSUPs, for short) are made with drop stitch material (woven or knitted) that connects the top (deck) shell and bottom (hull) layers together at a consistent thickness. Most iSUPs use six-inch-thick drop stitch material. Different densities and thicknesses are available, but most are usually coated with at least one layer of reinforced PVC. The layers are either glued or heat fused together. Fusion technology can reduce weight, improve performance, and may last longer than glued material.

REMEMBER

Thinner iSUPs have a lower center of gravity and lower volume rails that allow you to feel more connected to the water but also have more flex. Thicker iSUPs are generally more rigid.

An iSUP's top and bottom layers are joined along the rails with multiple strips of PVC or other materials that do the following:

>> Make the board airtight

>> Help shape the rocker curve of the board

>> May add some rigidity

The rail seams are either hand glued or heat fused (welded) together. Fusion is generally considered superior to gluing.

Graphics may be laminated or screen printed onto the PVC material before or after assembly. Lastly, a deck pad and external features are glued into place, including fixed fins or fin boxes, D-rings, handles, and additional layers of rigid materials or battens added to the rails to structurally stiffen the board.

Many inflatable boards come as a kit with a bag, paddle, and pump. These accessories are key to a good experience; a quality pump and paddle make a big difference to your ultimate satisfaction with your purchase.

Understanding hard board construction

Hard boards are usually made with a lightweight foam core (most commonly expanded polystyrene, or EPS), which is shaped and then wrapped with a durable outer shell made of fiberglass and epoxy. More premium construction options can also include layers of high-density PVC foam sandwiched over the lightweight foam core, and premium materials in the outer shell can include woven carbon fiber, Kevlar, Innegra, or molded polymer.

Some custom boards are still hand shaped by a master shaper, but most boards on the market are designed using computer-aided design. A shaping machine cuts the 3D shape out of a block of foam. The builder then finishes and smooths the computer shaped foam blank out by hand. Some mass-produced boards may also use molded foam blanks.

Different outer layers are then added over the light, fragile foam core to make it stronger. More advanced construction methods add an outer shell of wood veneer, honeycomb material, or high-density foam sheets, which are molded or vacuum bagged over the foam blank. An outer shell is then added using woven layers of fiberglass, carbon fiber, or similar materials that are laminated (coated) with epoxy.

The laminating epoxy is a two-part epoxy that's liquid when applied. It saturates the fibers and *cures* (turns solid) over time. Applying pressure and heat during the curing process can result in a stronger shell and improved bonding between the foam and outer shell.

Inserts such as fin boxes, handles, leash plugs, and other attachment points are added before the board is finished with layers of paint, graphics, and a clear coat. Finally, a deck pad is applied to the standing area.

Zeroing in on that Perfect Board

In this section, I look at the different types of boards available and how they're categorized:

>> All-around

>> Touring

>> Race

>> SUP surfing

Figure 3-1 gives you a good idea of how the types of boards I cover in the following sections differ.

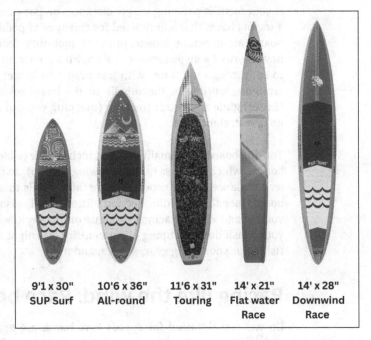

9'1 x 30"	10'6 x 36"	11'6 x 31"	14' x 21"	14' x 28"
SUP Surf	All-round	Touring	Flat water Race	Downwind Race

FIGURE 3-1: Different board types.

Rounding up the best features: All-around boards

The most common category of boards is the so-called *all-around board*, which — as you may have guessed — is designed to be pretty good at everything. These boards usually

>> Have a relatively flat bottom (planing hull)

>> Are in the 10-foot-to-11-foot-6-inch length range

>> Are 30 inches or wider

All-around boards are great for getting started because they're relatively stable and easy to paddle. You can use them for cruising and for riding waves, but they aren't optimized for either. They're great if you want your board to be able to do a bit of everything.

Going the distance: Touring boards

If your focus is paddling longer distances on flat water, consider a *touring board* that's optimized for this type of paddling. These boards are generally longer, in the 11-foot-to13-foot range and have more of a displacement shape with a pointy nose designed to cut through the water with less drag. The longer length and straighter outline in the middle of the board result in better (faster) glide and better tracking (meaning you can more easily go in a straight line).

Touring boards are usually 29 to 34 inches wide (wider than race boards, which I discuss in the following section), so they're easier to balance on and generally have thicker rails than all-round boards (see the preceding section). They usually also have more volume and extra attachment points on the deck, which allows you to lash down camping equipment for overnight adventures, fishing or snorkeling gear, snacks, and more.

Racing like the wind: Race boards

Do you feel the need for speed? *Race boards* are optimized for glide and speed in different conditions. They're longer than many other types (12 feet 6 inches and up); longer boards are usually faster because a longer *waterline* (the board length in the water) generally results in less drag and more speed. They're generally narrower (less than 28 inches wide) and more tippy than the touring boards in the preceding section and are designed for more advanced paddlers with good balance.

Most SUP races have different length classes for racing; the most common are 12 feet 6 inches, 14 feet, and Unlimited (over 14 feet).

Displacement hulls

Most race boards have displacement hulls with a pointy bow designed to split the water so it goes around the curvy rails and comes off the tail with minimal disruption. This shape aims to minimize drag at paddle speeds. Many modern race boards also have *dugouts* (recessed decks that lower the standing position for a lower center of gravity and better balance).

Planing hulls

In some places, including Hawaii, downwind racing is popular. In these races, competitors paddle with the wind and finish at a location downwind from the start, using the energy of the ocean and riding *wind swell* (bumps) along the way. Downwind race boards often have planing hulls designed to create lift from water going underneath the flat bottom and allowing the board to *plane* (skim over the water) at higher speeds when riding the bumps. Some unlimited (over 14 feet long) race boards may have a rudder system with a foot pedal that makes turning these otherwise unwieldy boards easier.

Riding the waves: SUP surfing boards

If you're most excited about catching and riding waves on your board, consider getting a board designed for SUP surfing. These boards are generally shorter (10 feet 6 inches or less), have more rocker (see Chapter 2), and sport a curvy outline that makes turning on a wave easier. The bottom is usually relatively flat with sharp rails in the tail that allow the board to speed up when you're taking off on a wave; you can turn the board by leaning into a turn. SUP surfing boards usually also have side fin boxes, which allow fin setups that provide extra hold when you're banking into carving turns. SUP surf boards come in different shapes and sizes, here are some commonly used categories of SUP surfing boards:

>> **Big Wave Guns** are made to catch big waves and perform in high-speed turns. They generally have a pointy nose and

tail (pintail), thinned out rails, a generous amount of rocker, and are relatively long (10 feet or longer) and narrow (29 inches or less).

>> **Longboard-style surf SUP's** mimic the characteristics of a traditional longboard surfboard with a focus on style, smooth flowing turns, cross stepping (moving up and down the board), and nose riding (where a surfer rides a wave with both on the nose of the board). They are usually longer (9 to 12 feet), have a wide, rounded nose, soft (rounded) rails, and a relatively narrow tail.

>> **Groveler SUP surf boards** are designed for riding in small, mushy, or weaker waves. They are usually shorter, wider, and thicker, with more volume and fuller rails. They also have a flatter rocker line and wider tail shapes, which helps generate speed and glide in smaller waves.

>> **High performance SUP surf boards** are made for advanced SUP surfers who want to push their limits as Zane Saenz demonstrates in Figure 3-2, riding in the barrel at Sunset Beach. They are shorter (7 to 9 feet), narrower, lower volume, with thinned out rails. Pro riders often use boards that don't have enough volume to float their own bodyweight, so they need to keep paddling to create dynamic lift from forward momentum to stay at the surface.

FIGURE 3-2: Zane Saenz at Sunset Beach.

With permission of Zane Saenz

AVOID BUYER'S REMORSE: TRY BEFORE YOU BUY!

A SUP isn't one size fits all! Nothing beats trying out as many boards as you can before committing to a purchase. Borrow boards from friends or attend paddle meetups or clinics where you can try out different boards. Many rental operations let you try different boards during your rental period, so take advantage of that option and compare the different boards they have. Keep track of the board lengths, widths, volumes, and shapes and how they differ. You'll soon find that some boards work much better for your needs than others. I encourage you to challenge yourself a bit; try boards that feel tippy at first because your balance skills will improve quickly. At the same time, you don't want to get a board that's so tippy you keep falling in and get frustrated. The main goal should be to have fun and get out on the water as much as possible.

The Search Is On: Finding the Right Board for You

So, you're ready to find a board that suits the conditions you plan to paddle in as well as your skills, height, weight, and future goals. The only thing to decide now is whether to get a brand-new board or a used one.

Buying a new board

A great way to buy the best board for your needs is to go to a store that specializes in selling standup paddle equipment and has a good selection of quality boards. Buying from a store with good customer support and from a reputable brand that backs its products can save you money and frustration in the long run. The store staff should be knowledgeable and trained to help steer you toward the perfect board. Talk to them about your needs and goals as well as which boards you've already tried and liked.

For your first board, you don't need to buy the highest-end, most-premium-construction model; save that money for your second or third board, when you know exactly what you want.

Many first-time buyers look for the cheapest board and a color they like. Although you certainly want a board that looks good and fits your budget, your first consideration should be that the board's dimensions, shape, and construction are right for your needs and goals.

Buying a used board

For your first board, you may want to consider a used board. If you paddle regularly, you may grow out of a beginner board quickly and want to move onto a higher-performance model. Assuming you really enjoy this sport, the first board you buy probably won't be the last, so starting with a less expensive, used beginner board can help you save toward a fancier new model later.

You can find many decent used beginner boards available for sale, as any quick look at online classified listings such as Facebook Marketplace and Craigslist shows. Many shops and board rental operations also sell used boards.

When buying a used board, carefully check for damage, repairs, and discoloration.

>> Boards with dings and cracks that weren't promptly repaired may have taken on water that seeped into the foam core, making them noticeably heavier. Moisture and salt inside the core are difficult to remove and can cause other issues, such as *delamination* (when the outer layer separates from the foam core).

>> Check for small cracks around the fin boxes and inserts and for other signs of damage.

>> The nose, tail, and rails of the board are especially prone to dings and cracks that may leak water.

>> Don't buy a used inflatable board without fully inflating it and making sure it doesn't have any slow leaks. Inflatables with a leak along the rail seams usually aren't worth repairing.

Chapter **4**

Paddle Perfection: Finding a Match to Propel You Forward

The paddle is often an afterthought. It is often included for free with a board purchase and many just make do with whatever they get. While choosing the right board is important, the paddle should not be overlooked as it has a big impact on the overall performance. It is what propels you forward efficiently; you can think of it as your motor. Much like a master Samurai takes great care in choosing and wielding his blade, a good paddler is skillful in propelling and maneuvering the board using their carefully chosen paddle.

One of my first paddles was a beautiful hand-crafted wood paddle and I loved it. Unfortunately, the wood shaft started fatiguing and broke after about a year. Since then, I have been using carbon fiber paddles for the strength and light weight.

A Good Paddle — Like a Samurai's Sword

To love your paddle, you must first get to know it. Figure 4-1 gets you on the right track by listing the different parts of a paddle and their functions, while the following list explains each part.

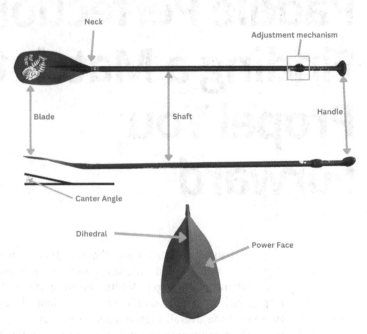

FIGURE 4-1: The parts of a paddle.

>> **Blade:** The *blade* is the flat part that goes into the water. Paddles have different blade sizes and shapes. You can think of the blade size like the gears on a bike. A smaller blade is like a lower gear, so it accelerates well, can be

paddled at a higher cadence, and works better for lighter paddlers. Smaller blades also tend to be lighter, narrower, less likely to bang into the rails, and easier on your shoulders.

Conversely, a bigger blade is like a higher gear on a bike. It has more power, and you can paddle it at a lower pace. Bigger blades are suitable for heavier, more powerful paddlers, but bigger isn't necessarily better. Personally, I prefer using smaller blades. I feel like they're more efficient and put less strain on my body.

>> **Power face:** The *power face* is the side of the paddle that pushes against the water and faces you when you're paddling forward. It's usually slightly curved toward you.

>> **Canter:** The angle between the blade and the shaft is the *canter*. The blade is usually *cantered* (angled forward) by 8 to 15 degrees to give it a more efficient angle on the water when applying power during the stroke. Beginners often intuitively hold the blade backward, thinking it will "scoop" more water. (More on that Chapter 10.)

>> **Dihedral:** Many blades have a *dihedral* (raised ridge) on the power face that directs the water to either side to prevent *flutter* (side-to-side motion while paddling).

>> **Neck:** The *neck* is where the blade connects to the shaft.

>> **Shaft:** The *shaft* is the long pole between the blade and the handle. Most shafts are round and straight, though some have an oval shape and some are tapered, with a smaller diameter at the top and a bigger diameter at the bottom. Generally, smaller-diameter and oval-shaped shafts are more comfortable to grip, especially for folks with smaller hands. Shafts vary in flexibility depending on what they're made of as well as the diameter and shape of the shaft. A flexible shaft is more forgiving, while a stiffer shaft is generally more efficient and powerful.

>> **Handle:** The top of the paddle where you grip the paddle with your top hand is the *handle*. Most handles have a flatter side facing your palm and a more curved part for your fingers to wrap over.

A longer paddle (8 to 16 inches taller than you) allows you to stand more upright and reach farther forward, while a shorter paddle allows you to apply more power to the blade. SUP surfers (and also racers) often prefer a shorter paddle (up to 8 inches taller than them) that allows for quick acceleration, better leverage on the blade, and easier handling when switching the paddle from one side of the board to the other.

Figure 4-2 shows a few methods for determining the right paddle length for you.

>> A good starting point to determine a comfortable length is "a shaka over the head," which is about 6 to 8 inches overhead, as you can see in Figure 4-2a. (And, yes, the *shaka* or "hang loose" sign is now the official state gesture of Hawaii, so it's a totally appropriate description for paddle length.)

>> The "wrist over handle" method (Figure 4-2b) results in an 8-to-12-inch overhead length, which works well for cruising in a more upright position.

>> The "upside down" method (Figure 4-2c) also works well because it accounts for the blade shape. With the paddle placed upside down, the neck of the blade should be around eye level. (I cover the neck and other paddle parts in the preceding section.)

REMEMBER

When paddling comfortably with the blade fully submerged in the water, your top hand on the handle should be right about at eye level, as Figure 4-3 illustrates.

FIGURE 4-2: Three methods to determine proper paddle length.

FIGURE 4-3:
Handle at
eye level
while
paddling.

Adjustable paddles are helpful when you're starting out because you can experiment with different heights and see what works best for you. (For more on adjustable paddles see the "Finding the Perfect Fit: Adjustable versus Fixed Length Paddles" section later in this chapter.)

REMEMBER

You also need to take the thickness of the board into consideration when choosing a paddle length. On a very thick, high-volume board, you may be standing several inches higher above the water surface than you would be on a thin, low-volume board, so your paddle length needs to be longer on a thicker board to account for that difference. Flip to Chapter 3 for details on board thickness.

THE DANGERS OF AN IMPROPERLY SIZED PADDLE

If the paddle is too short, you must lean forward and/or bend your knees more to plant the blade into the water. This shift can result in unnecessary board movement, loss of balance, and lower back pain.

If the paddle is too long, your top arm and elbow must reach up too high over your shoulder. Repeatedly lifting your elbow above eye level can result in rotator cuff injuries. A long paddle also means that your bottom hand is farther away from the blade, resulting in less leverage and control.

Comparing Paddle Construction and Paddle Weights

Paddles come in several materials, including the following:

>> **Aluminum** shafts with a molded plastic blade are generally the least expensive. They're rigid and relatively strong, but they're also heavier than paddles made with other materials.

>> **Fiberglass** shafts and blades are a step up from aluminum/plastic. They have more flex than aluminum paddles, so they act like a shock absorber for your shoulders, but they can also be less efficient. Fiberglass is usually a bit heavier but also less expensive than a full carbon paddle.

>> **Carbon** is considered the best material for paddles as I write this; it's light, strong, and stiff. A good carbon paddle is very light, which makes paddling more efficient. (As an added bonus, lifting the paddle after every stroke is easier on your shoulders.)

WARNING

Some "carbon" paddles are really fiberglass with just one thin layer of carbon on the surface for looks, so make sure you know what you're getting for your money. A well designed, full-carbon paddle can be quite expensive but it's a worthwhile investment.

REMEMBER

The weight of the paddle is much more noticeable than the weight of the board when you're out on the water, since you are lifting the paddle with every stroke, so investing some time and money into a good paddle is definitely worthwhile.

Finding the Perfect Fit: Adjustable versus Fixed Length Paddles

As I note earlier in the chapter, some SUP paddles are adjustable, while the lengths of others are fixed. In the following sections, I break down those options (as well as the adjustable's cousin, the travel paddle).

Feeling out fixed length paddles

Fixed length paddles have a straight shaft that's cut to the proper length, and the handle is glued into it. If you're buying from a specialty store able to size, cut, and glue a fixed length paddle for you, you should consider this option.

A fixed length paddle has several advantages if you're interested in a high-performance paddle for your own use — that is, you don't have to share it — and you know your preferred paddle length. (The earlier section "Evaluating Paddle Length" helps you figure out that measurement.)

>> The handle is glued into the shaft at the correct length, so the paddle is watertight and requires no maintenance. You don't have to worry about the paddle taking on water and possibly sinking, and you don't need to rinse it with fresh water after use.

>> Fixed paddles are usually lighter weight and have a more consistent flex pattern than adjustable paddles (see the following section), resulting in the best performance if you don't need adjustability.

>> The smooth shaft has no joints or bumps, which also allows your lower hand to slide up on the shaft when you're changing sides with the paddle.

Some fixed paddles (such as my company's Blue Planet Kai Zen V3) have extended handles that are hot glued into the shaft. This makes the length semi-adjustable by heating the joint with a heat gun to soften the glue and extending or shortening the handle.

Assessing adjustable length paddles

As the name suggests, you can change *adjustable length* paddles to the correct length by using a lever or snap adjustment. If you're buying a board as a package deal, it usually comes with an adjustable paddle because that's the most convenient option for the seller.

If you aren't sure what length works best for you or if you're sharing the paddle with others, an adjustable paddle is your best bet.

The obvious advantage of an adjustable paddle is that you can fine tune the length, even on the fly while paddling. For example, you can make the paddle longer for cruising in a more upright position and shorten the length when paddling into the wind in a more crouched position. It's also ideal for sharing with others, if you are just not sure yet what size paddle you prefer, or if you want to use the paddle for different disciplines and using it with different boards.

These paddles do have some downsides:

>> They can take on water and weigh a bit more if you leave them floating for a long time. On an adjustable paddle, the handle extension tube and adjustment system also add weight.

>> The telescoping shaft affects the flex pattern because it's stiffer where the tubes are doubled up and creates a pressure point on the shaft where it transitions from two tubes to one.

>> On some round adjustable paddles, the handle can rotate if the adjustment clamp isn't tight enough. Some adjustable paddles are oval shaped or use a notch to keep the handle from rotating. (Trust me, you don't want the handle to rotate.)

WARNING

>> If you're using an adjustable paddle in salt water, you need to rinse it regularly with fresh water after use by completely removing the extension piece and rinsing the inside of the shaft. Adjustable paddles can build up a layer of salt, sand, and corrosion between the tubes and seize up.

>> If your adjustable paddle has a clamp system, you may need to tighten the screws occasionally to maintain a tight fit.

A variation of the adjustable paddle is the three-piece *travel paddle*. Often used with inflatable boards (see Chapter 3), these are very convenient to transport, but the extra joint adds weight and affects the flex pattern. On some travel paddles the joints also wiggle a bit, so you're looking at a trade-off between convenience and performance.

IN THIS CHAPTER

» **Keeping connected to your board (and your paddling mates)**

» **Perusing personal flotation devices**

» **Getting to know important communication tools**

» **Backing up your safety gear with extra equipment**

Chapter **5**

Safety Dance: Take a Chance, but Don't Leave the World Behind

Standup paddleboarding is exhilarating, but a fun day on the water can quickly turn life-threatening. In this chapter, I fill you in on the safety features and equipment that can help bail you out of a dicey situation.

REMEMBER

Safety equipment is important regardless of your experience level but especially for beginners. Here in Hawaii, I regularly see inexperienced paddlers heading out in offshore trade winds thinking "this is easy" when actually the wind is pushing them along. The trouble is that when they eventually turn around, they realize to their horror that paddling back to shore against the wind (or current) can be very challenging.

Your Best Friends: Wearing a Leash and Using the Buddy System

Sure, doing things that are a bit out of your comfort zone is thrilling, but ultimately water isn't a natural environment for humans. You can only swim and hold your breath for so long, so you need to be aware of the risks that come with SUP and take steps to minimize them.

Leashes save lives: Keeping contact with your board

One of the greatest risks in standup paddleboarding is becoming separated from your board while being far offshore. The board is your most important piece of safety equipment. It's a big floatation device that will carry you back to shore safely if you use it properly.

For that reason, using a good leash to connect yourself to your board is essential. If you fall off your board and you don't have a leash, even a light breeze can be enough to blow the board away from you faster than you can swim to catch up to it. So, yes, you should *always* wear a leash.

WARNING

The leash should be as long as the board. A leash shorter than that can be dangerous because the board is too close to you when you fall in waves and can trip you when you're falling forward, which can cause you to hit your board.

Looking at the leash types

Leash lines are made of urethane and are available in different thicknesses. Thin, lightweight leashes are suitable for calm conditions, while thick, heavy-duty leashes work for use in bigger waves and strong wings. The two main types of leash lines are coiled leashes and straight leashes; here are some pointers on which to choose for your needs.

>> **Coiled leashes** are great for cruising because they don't drag behind the board and slow your progress. They're also less likely to catch on rocks, seaweed, kelp, or other things floating in the water. I don't recommend using them in waves because they can get stretched out when a wave drags the board. Overstretching can quickly turn a coiled leash into a tangled, limp mess that you need to replace.

>> **Straight leashes** are ideal for surfing; they hold up well even if repeatedly stretched out. They also minimize recoil so the board is less likely to snap back toward your head after getting pulled by a wave. The downsides are the additional drag when you're paddling and the fact that they're more likely to catch on things floating in the water.

Choosing your leash connection

The basic type of leash (see the preceding section) isn't the only thing to be concerned about. You also need a way to attach that leash (and by extension the board) to you somehow. Here are the mechanics:

>> **Cuffs:** Most leashes use *ankle cuffs*, which attach around your ankle with the leash sticking out to the side. When you're just learning to paddle, you can wear the leash on either foot, but if you're planning to catch waves, put it on the back foot. (More on that in Chapter 13.) Less common cuffs connect around the calf under the knee or around the waist. Attaching the leash around the calf or waist can make stepping on the leash less likely when moving around the board.

>> **Quick-release leashes:** These leashes allow you to quickly disconnect the board in an emergency. If you're paddling on a river with strong currents, use a waist belt leash with a quick-release pull tab. If the leash catches on a submerged object, you may not be able to reach your ankle to remove the leash in a strong current.

>> **Board attachment:** The leash attaches to the board using a leash string attached to a leash plug on the tail of the board. Most leashes have a hook-and-loop "rail saver" strap (see Figure 5-1) that attaches to the leash string and protects the rail. Make sure to fully open this strap, loop it over the leash string, and firmly attach the fastener over it.

TIP

I remove the leash from the board for transport and storage but always leave the leash string attached to the board. You should do the same.

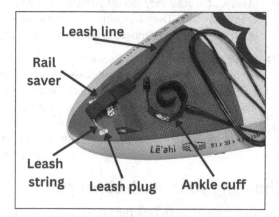

Leash line

Rail saver

Leash string

Leash plug

Ankle cuff

Lē'ahi

FIGURE 5-1:
Leash parts.

Focusing on leash failure

WARNING

Leashes can fail. Here are some of the most common causes of leash failure:

>> **Closure coming undone:** If the fastener strap on the ankle cuff or board attachment is applied improperly, worn out, or clogged with debris or sand, it may get disconnected.

>> **Leash string failure:** Regularly check your leash string; make sure the knot is tied tightly and replace the leash string if it starts to fray.

>> **Leash line failure:** Make sure the thickness of the urethane leash you're using is suitable for the conditions. The urethane material and connection points degrade over time and can get brittle, especially if you haven't used the line for a long time or it has been exposed to sun and heat. Replace leashes that are more than five years old.

Introducing the buddy system

SUP is a solo sport, but it's also a social activity. Sharing the experience with others is always more fun. It's also much safer because you can look out for each other, provide help, and call for rescue in case of emergency.

REMEMBER

When paddling with others, always make sure that you keep everyone in sight and that everyone returns to shore safely.

If you must go out by yourself, carefully assess the risks. Share your *float plan* (where and when you plan to paddle) with someone on shore and check in with them when you get back safely. Be prepared to self-rescue, if necessary; carry safety gear, including a communication device (I discuss those later in the chapter), and take precautions to minimize the risks.

Staying Afloat: Personal Floatation Devices

On inland waterways and almost anywhere in the United States and internationally, SUPs are considered vessels, and you're required to have an approved personal floatation device, or PFD. (The exception: In Hawaii, the Coast Guard considers standup paddleboards surf craft and doesn't enforce life jacket usage as long as you use a leash. You can read about those in the earlier section "Your Best Friends: Wearing a Leash and Using the Buddy System.") Make sure to know your local rules and, if in doubt, use a PFD. In many locations, officials strictly enforce the rule with citations and fines.

REMEMBER

Regardless of the rules, if you aren't a strong swimmer, you should always wear a (non-inflatable) PFD and only paddle close to shore in protected waters. Ideally, work on your swimming skills first and make sure you're comfortable swimming longer distances unassisted before getting into SUP in the first place.

REMEMBER

A signaling device, such as a whistle, should be attached to any PFD. Head to the later section "Looking at Other Emergency Equipment" for more on signaling devices.

Stating the obvious: Use your common sense

REMEMBER

You should wear a PFD on your body, not have it attached to the board. Most places' boating rules state that a PFD has to be accessible on the vessel. As I note earlier in the chapter, getting separated from the board is the greatest risk; although having a PFD attached to your board may comply with the rules, doing so is definitely unsafe. Even if you don't get separated from the board, removing the PFD from the board and putting it on may be a real challenge in an actual emergency.

If you're a strong swimmer and want to do the minimum required to comply with the requirement, small, unobtrusive inflatable PFD waist packs are available. They usually have a CO_2 cartridge that inflates the vest with a pull of the string. (See what I say about these kinds of PFDs in the following section.)

Evaluating the five types of PFDs

The U.S. Coast Guard recognizes the following five types of PFDs (check them out in Figure 5-2):

>> **Type I:** These devices are offshore life jackets; they're best for open, rough, or remote waters. They're designed to turn most unconscious wearers face up in the water and provide the most buoyancy (at least 22 pounds).

REMEMBER

PFD buoyancy refers to the amount of floatation provided. The level of buoyancy required depends on the wearer's weight, body composition, and water conditions. Since the human body is naturally buoyant, it does not take much buoyancy to keep someone afloat.

>> **Type II:** Type II PFDs are near-shore buoyant vests. They're designed for calmer waters and will turn some unconscious wearers face-up, but they don't perform as consistently as Type I vests.

TIP

>> **Type III:** The most common type of PFD used for standup paddleboarding is Type III. These flotation aids are suitable for conscious users in calm, near-shore waters and provide a minimum of 15.5 pounds of buoyancy.

WARNING

>> **Type IV:** These throwable devices are intended to be thrown to a person in distress. Type IV devices aren't recommended for use on a SUP because they are designed to hold onto but not to swim with.

>> **Type V:** Type V PFDs are special-use devices and include inflatable models such as the waist packs I mention in the preceding section. You must use them according to the instructions. They may provide performance equivalent to Type I, II, or III PFDs depending on their design.

TIP

Some things to consider before purchasing an inflatable PFD:

>> They use CO_2 cartridges, which you can't take on commercial flights (say, if you want to paddle the seven seas).

>> The cartridge needs to be properly armed to be functional.

>> Putting the inflated vest over your head may be challenging in an emergency.

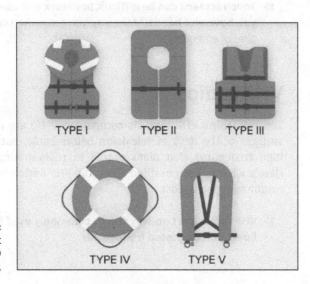

FIGURE 5-2: U.S. Coast Guard PFD designations.

Sending Out an SOS: Communication Gear

Anytime you plan to paddle farther from shore than you can comfortably swim back, you should carry a communication device. The following sections look at some of the most common options.

Cellphones

They're not just for land use anymore! Just keep the following in mind:

>> **Carrying a cellphone in near-shore waters that have good cell coverage is very effective, both to communicate with other paddlers and to call for help.** Double-check whether coverage is available where you intend to paddle (and make sure your phone is charged).

>> **Although some cellphones are waterproof, salt water can damage charge ports.** Keep any cellphone in a waterproof bag or case — just in case.

>> **Touch screens can be difficult to unlock and use when you have wet hands.** Make sure you can make a call in case of emergency.

VHF radios

You may think VHF (and its companion UHF) are just ancient vestiges of the days of television before cable, but VHF (very high frequency) also plays a role in radio communications. Here's what to keep in mind about the VHF option for your SUP communication needs:

>> **VHF radios are two-way radios commonly used by boats on designated frequencies.**

> **>> Channel 16 is the international channel for distress calls.** Other channels are available for reliable communication with other paddlers and boats over relatively short distances even if no cellphone service is available.

Beacons of hope: ePIRBs

Automated distress signals are an option for SUP emergencies. An *emergency position–indicating radio beacon* (ePIRBs) may be just the ticket. When activated, these emergency beacons transmit a distress signal with exact GPS location via satellite.

Here are a couple of other things to know about ePIRBS:

>> ePIRBs don't require paid satellite network service, but for use in the United States, you do need to register them with the federal government at www.noaa.gov. (If you're paddling internationally, check out the local requirements ahead of time.)

>> ePIRBS are designed for maritime use. They are waterproof and provide peace of mind and a way to call for help in case of emergencies while at sea or in remote locations; just keep in mind that they don't provide two-way communication.

Satellite communication devices

If you're the kind of person who thinks "the remoter, the better," then you really should consider opting for a communication system that ditches cellphone towers for eyes in the sky. Yes, I'm talking satellites. Devices that rely on satellites have the following characteristics:

>> They can send a distress signal and provide two-way text or voice communication via satellites.

>> These devices are the best option for communication in remote areas where cellphone service isn't available.

>> They require a monthly or annual service plan to communicate via satellite networks.

Looking at Other Emergency Equipment

I cover a lot of tools you can use to attract attention from nearby vessels or search parties in the preceding sections, but frankly, even your safety equipment benefits from the buddy system. You should carry one or more of the following in addition to a communication device, especially when venturing farther offshore. (Head to the earlier section "Sending Out an SOS: Communication Gear" for more on those items.)

>> Whistle

>> Signal mirror

>> Handheld flare

>> Distress flag

>> Floating streamer

REMEMBER

Although carrying a full first aid kit while paddling may not be practical, having a suitable one in your car or on shore to clean and cover cuts is a good idea.

DON'T WORRY; BE HAPPY

Talking about safety may make you feel a bit anxious. Respecting Mother Nature, being aware of possible risks, and mitigating those risks as much as possible is a good idea. Don't let that stop you from enjoying an adventure on the water though.

When I learned to windsurf on Maui, I had a debilitating fear of sharks. Every time I fell into the water, I was expecting sharks to attack me at any moment. It took me several years, but I've overcome this fear.

These are some things that have helped me and may help you combat whatever fear is getting between you and paddling:

- **Learn about the scary thing.** In my case, it was finding out more about sharks and realizing that they aren't out to get me.

- **Research the odds and rationalize the risk.** For example, sharks kill only about five or six people a year worldwide, while thousands drown in rip currents annually.

- **Go where others are in the water.** Seeing others having fun in the water can help you feel more comfortable as you realize the risk of, say, a shark attack is minimal.

- **Take deep breaths and try to relax to reduce fear and anxiety.**

If you share my *galeophobia* (fear of sharks), follow this link to watch a video titled "Overcoming the fear of sharks so you can enjoy the ocean."

www.youtube.com/watch?v=P2FfJ24Y9cU

Chapter 6

Shielding Yourself from the Elements

Water is the most obvious element you encounter in standup paddleboarding, but it isn't the only one you have to contend with. The air and water temperature and sun exposure also play a part in your paddling experience. In this chapter, I help you suit up and cover up so you can enjoy your paddle even in less-than-idyllic conditions.

Dressing for Success: Weather, Temperature, and Conditions

Although being cold while paddling is uncomfortable, overheating can be an issue as well, especially during physical exertion. That's why you need to choose the right kind and amount of clothing to protect you from the elements depending on the conditions.

On my visit to Tofino, British Columbia, Canada, one February, the waves were pumping, and many folks (including lots of SUP surfers) were out on the water having a great time. The air and water temperature were very cold, especially compared to what I was used to in Hawaii. Luckily, I found a shop that offered both SUP and wet suit rentals as well as a heated changing room with hot showers. I ended up having a fantastic time and was surprisingly comfortable wearing a thick wet suit, booties, gloves, and a hood. (See me fully suited up in Figure 6-1.)

FIGURE 6-1: Your author, fully suited up in Tofino, B.C., Canada.

Paddling in cold weather: Wet suits versus dry suits

Whether you choose a wet suit or a dry suit largely depends on how much water you want to keep out. I discuss each suit in the following sections. You can see an overview of the different types of wet suits (full and shorty) and dry suits available in Figure 6-2.

FIGURE 6-2: Types of wet suits and dry suits available.

PNG-Universe/ Adobe Stock Photos   *Min Wan/Adobe Stock Photos*   *MarekPhotoDesign.com/ Adobe Stock Photos*

Wet suits

Hugh Bradner, a UC Berkely physicist, is often credited with inventing the modern wet suit in 1952. *Wet suits* are made of flexible, tight-fitting *neoprene* (synthetic rubber) material and provide thermal protection while wet. Body heat warms the small amount of water that can enter the suit, and that heated water regulates the temperature. A wet suit also helps protect you from abrasion, UV light, and stings from marine organisms and provides extra buoyancy.

TIP

Wet suits come in different configurations and thicknesses. Thicker, full-coverage wet suits are made for cold water. Thinner suits that may not cover the full body are for more temperate conditions and likely aren't suitable (pun intended) for paddling in cold weather.

REMEMBER

If you find yourself overheating, you can jump in and allow some cold water to enter the wet suit to regulate the temperature.

To be effective, a wet suit should be tight-fitting. A properly fitting suit can be challenging to put on and off, so you should definitely try a suit on in person before buying it to make sure it's a good fit. The neoprene material and seams vary in quality and amount of stretch. As with all equipment, purchasing from a reputable brand with good quality and an extended warranty is worthwhile.

Dry suits

Where wet suits keep out most water (see the preceding section), *dry suits* are designed to completely seal out the water with tight-fitting cuffs around the wrists, ankles, and neck. You climb into the suit; slide your head, feet, and hands through the tight-fitting cuffs; and then seal the suit with the waterproof zipper. Inside the suit, you can layer clothing depending on the conditions.

REMEMBER

Dry suits are great for paddling in cold weather in relatively calm conditions. However, I don't recommend them for rough conditions or in the surf where wipeouts and getting tumbled by waves can cause water to enter the suit through the cuffs (despite the design).

Dry suits generally don't allow sweat and moisture to escape, so use moisture wicking layers close to the skin and clothing that insulates well even when wet, such as synthetic or wool layers. Down jackets are warm when dry but lose much of their insulation when wet, so down insulation isn't good to wear under a dry suit.

Keeping your extremities warm

Wet suits and dry suits (see the preceding sections) cover your body but not your feet, hands, and head. So even with the warm-est of suits, hands and feet can quickly get cold and go numb. Covering up those extremities can keep that from happening.

Foot coverings

Your feet are part the most likely to get wet and stay wet when paddling, so for cold water, you should wear neoprene booties. Like wet suits for your feet, they're available in different thick-nesses and should be tight-fitting and comfortable and have a grippy sole.

In warmer weather, booties or water shoes aren't necessary; personally, I prefer paddling barefoot for a direct connection to the board. Many people wear water shoes to protect their feet from sharp rocks and reefs on the sea bottom when falling in or while entering and exiting the water. Good water shoes should fit snugly and allow water and sand to drain out easily. Thick, padded soles can provide extra cushioning, but I prefer using thin, grippy soles that provide a more direct board feel.

Water shoes are often called "reef walkers," but you should never use them to walk on live reefs. Reefs are fragile living things, and you should never walk on live ones, regardless of whether you wear shoes.

Gloves

Neoprene gloves do a good job of keeping your hands warm. Because you're using them to grip the paddle, make sure they're suitable for paddling — that is, they have a durable, abrasion-resistant grip surface.

SUNBURN IS NOT A GOOD LOOK

If you're fair skinned and have enjoyed a lifetime of outdoor sports as I have, you already know all about the damage the sun can cause to your skin. If you're still young, carefree, and looking to get a tan, beware of the long-term damage to your skin. Skin cancer is the most common form of cancer globally. Although the most common skin cancers can be removed if caught early, melanoma is a form of skin cancer that's more likely to spread to other parts of the body and can be very serious if not detected and treated early.

Tip: Regular skin checks and early detection are crucial in reducing the risk of skin cancer and improving treatment outcomes.

Paddling gloves are also available for use in warm weather and can protect your hands from blisters and provide sun protection. Personally, I find that paddling gloves used for long-distance paddling can help prevent blisters but can also cause uncomfortable chafing, so I use only neoprene gloves to keep my hands warm if necessary.

Covering up is the best protection: Sun-protective clothing

Sunscreens and sunblock can help protect you from the sun, but you need to reapply them regularly . . . and even then you can still get a sunburn if you aren't careful. Wearing long-sleeved shirts, pants, and a brimmed hat is the best way to protect yourself from harmful rays. (I also suggest avoiding the peak UV hours in the middle of the day, if possible.)

Although you can still get sunburned through a wet cotton T-shirt, most synthetic tops made for watersports provide better protection than even the most powerful sunblock. A long-sleeved top offers good protection for your upper body and arms, and a hood can provide neck protection as well.

TIP

Make sure your shirt's sleeves are long enough and don't ride up. Some shirts have a hole for your thumb, which can help keep the sleeves in place. (That way, your wrists and part of your hands stay covered.)

If you're going out in the surf or in windy conditions, a tight-fitting Lycra shirt works best. On the other hand, a looser-fitting shirt can be more comfortable for cruising. In hot conditions, light colors and breathable fabrics keep you cooler; just make sure the fabric effectively blocks UV rays. I prefer wearing shorts, but light synthetic pants or tights can protect your legs so you have very little of your skin exposed to direct sunlight.

To complete your sun protection, add a hat to your paddling wardrobe. A baseball-style hat with a rigid brim can provide protection for your eyes and face, but a hat with a full, wrap-around brim also protects the sides of your face and neck. If you choose a full-brim hat, make sure it's made for watersports and has a stiff brim that doesn't flop in your face when wet. Personally, I like the Shelta brand hats with "no flop" brim, but many other good hats are available. Look for a stiff brim and a strap to keep it in place when you fall in.

Lathering Up: Sunscreen, Sunblock, and SPF

Even if you cover most parts of your body with clothing of some type, you need to protect any skin that's still exposed to UV rays on a sunny day. The terms *sunscreen* and *sunblock* are often used interchangeably, but they have some differences: The chemicals in sunscreen typically absorb UV radiation, while sunblock contains minerals like zinc oxide or titanium dioxide that physically block the UV rays.

For that reason, sunblock is usually thicker and more visible on the skin than sunscreen and tends (in my experience) to be more water resistant. It's also less likely to run and irritate the eyes, which is why I prefer using thicker sunblock on my face. For my legs and other exposed body parts, I prefer thinner sunscreen that's easier to apply and spread.

Because you're likely to get wet when paddling, choose sunscreen labeled "water resistant," which is formulated to provide protection for 40 to 80 minutes, even when wet, before you need to reapply it. Choose a broad-spectrum formula that protects against both UVA and UVB rays and opt for a high SPF (sun protection factor) rating — I'm talking 30 or higher — to ensure maximum protection.

Your best bet is to apply sunscreen to clean, dry skin and wait at least ten minutes to let the sunscreen absorb before getting wet. Otherwise, much of it can wash off. Make sure to cover all exposed body parts, especially those facing the sun, and don't forget your neck, the backs of your hands, and the tops of your feet.

Some sunscreens can make your hands slip on the paddle, so washing your hands with soap after lathering up and before grabbing your paddle or other gear is a good idea. Also be careful when applying sunscreen to your feet and shins; it can transfer to your deck pad when you kneel on it and make the board slippery to stand on. Sunscreen and sunblock labeled "sport" tend to be less slippery.

WARNING

Some sunscreen ingredients, like oxybenzone, have been found to be damaging to coral reefs and marine environments and aren't allowed in some places, including Hawaii. Please make sure to use sunscreens labeled "reef safe."

WEARING GLASSES ON THE WATER

If you don't have to wear prescription glasses, avoiding wearing glasses when going out on the water is usually best. An unexpected fall can mean the glasses slip right off your face and sink to the bottom before you even notice that they're missing. (Even if you don't lose them, wet glasses can be hard to see through.)

If you need to wear glasses, make sure to secure them with a floating tether. Neoprene tethers work well; just make sure they fit tightly over the glasses and do a float test to make sure the tether floats your glasses if they fall in the water. Some brands make floating sunglasses; Bombers and Dragon are two that come to mind. Floating glasses with polarized lenses are a good choice if you need sunglasses to protect your eyes.

Chapter **7**

Preparing for the Big Blue

One of the reasons many surfers are weary of all the newbie stand up paddleboarders out there on the water is because these beginner paddlers head straight out, thinking they can catch and ride waves the first time out. They then end up flailing around out of control in the surf zone and endangering others in the lineup with their big boards.

Don't be that person! As I explain in this chapter, you want to look for calm water and stay far away from any waves when you're learning the stand up paddleboarding ropes. You'll have a much better experience (and so will those around you!). I also give you tips on monitoring the weather conditions and making sure you're properly fed and hydrated ahead of your excursion. Finally, I suggest some balance, cross-training, and breathing exercises that can help keep you in top SUP shape.

Just Chillin': Taking Baby Steps

The ideal conditions for your first attempts are very calm water on a protected waterway (a small lake, for example); either that, or you just stay close to shore. You want to avoid wind, rough and choppy water, waves, and currents. A windy day makes learning particularly challenging because keeping the board pointed into the wind and making progress when paddling upwind take some skill. The wind also whips up chop, and the rough water makes balancing on the board more difficult.

Beginners who go out on a windy day without instruction tend to get blown straight downwind and think, "this is a breeze, I got this"; then they try to turn around and paddle back to where they started. At this point, they realize that paddling upwind is much more challenging than going with the wind (or with the current). I cover some tips for paddling in windy conditions, currents, and waves in Part 2, but do yourself a favor and look for calm conditions when you're first starting out.

Checking the lay of the land (well, water)

Before you decide to paddle out, take some time to assess the weather conditions.

>> What do the trees and the clouds tell you about the wind direction and gust levels?

>> Do you see dark clouds moving in? Does the weather look like it may be changing?

>> How much daylight do you have before sunset, and are you dressed properly for the air and water temperature (and wind chill)?

Now look at the water. Is the surface smooth, or does it have small ripples? If the water is rough or you can see *whitecaps* (waves whose crests show white foam), you should avoid going out if you're still a beginner.

TIP

A very calm, slow-moving river can be a good place to start, but avoid any current when learning.

If you're at the ocean, also investigate whether you have an easy entry and exit point without any breaking waves. Is the tide coming in or going out? Are there shallow areas or hazards to avoid? Talk to local paddlers and ask them for tips. Most are happy to help you out with some pointers.

WARNING

An outgoing tide can cause strong currents that can pull you out to sea, especially at river mouths and *estuaries* (where the fresh river currents meet the salty tide). If you ever do get caught in a rip current or tidal current, don't exhaust yourself paddling against the current; rather, paddle parallel to shore until you get out of the current, and then paddle back to shore.

REMEMBER

Check the conditions and forecast before going into the water. Nothing beats observing the conditions in person, but I also like to check them remotely (before driving to the beach) by using online tools. The following list highlights some of the apps and websites I use in addition to regular weather forecasts before going into the water:

>> **Wind:** www.windguru.cz/53. Type your desired location into the search bar. (**Note:** Information for some locations requires a paid account.)

>> **Wind, wave, and weather conditions and forecast:** www.surfline.com/.

>> **Wind:** The Windy.com website (www.windy.com) or its phone app (available for Apple and Android devices).

>> **Hawaii-specific surf conditions:** www.surfnewsnetwork.com/.

>> **Tides:** Tide Charts phone app (apple and android), or Tide Alert phone app (apple only).

Eating right to stay upright

Fueling your body properly makes your paddle adventure more enjoyable. I try to avoid paddling on a full stomach and like to eat a healthy, easily digestible meal at least 30 minutes before going on the water. You know best what foods you digest easily and which ones agree with you; I, for example, avoid deep fried foods.

GETTING FIT AND HAVING FUN

If you hope to get fit and shed some body fat while having fun on the water, you aren't alone. Standup paddleboarding is not only fun but also a full-body workout. I've both experienced the health benefits myself and heard from many others in the same boat (or board). At my SUP business (Blue Planet), we regularly get firsthand reports from customers that paddling on a regular basis and eating a healthy diet resulted in lower body fat, more muscle mass, better fitness and balance, and improved overall physical and mental well-being. Unlike exercising in a gym, these benefits aren't just from burning calories; they're a result of unplugging from the daily grind, plugging into nature, engaging the whole body, being present and focused on balancing, and being close to the water.

If I'm planning to paddle for more than 30 minutes or so, I bring some water (plain water or water with some electrolytes mixed in) to stay hydrated. I like to wear a hydration pack with a tube that makes drinking while paddling easy. If I'm planning to paddle for more than an hour, I also bring some energy bars to refuel.

REMEMBER

Energy bars and gels are convenient because they have water-proof wrapping and are easy to eat and digest while on the water. I try to avoid food with high sugar content because it gives a rush of energy that tends to wear off quickly.

From Novice to Ninja: Balance Training and Staying Fit Off the Water

Whether you want to get ready for your first time on the water or just want to stay in shape, the following sections dig into some land-based ways you can prepare for paddling without getting wet.

Training your balance

I've heard people say, "I have terrible balance," but the good news is that you can train and improve your balance through practice. Much like weight training can make your muscles stronger, balance training can improve your balancing ability.

REMEMBER

Standing on a tippy board is excellent balance training. As I mention in Chapter 2, a wider board is more stable than a narrower board. The more challenging balancing on a board is, the more your balance will improve. That's why I encourage paddlers to get a board that's challenging to balance on but not so tippy that you constantly fall in, get frustrated, and don't keep paddling.

In the following sections, I go over ways to train your balance on land.

Working with balance trainers

Many types of balance trainers are available that can help improve your balance, coordination, stamina, and leg strength — all great ways to prepare for SUP and to stay in shape during the off-season.

>> **Rolling with roller boards:** The most common balance boards consist of a round roller with a hard plank on top. You start with one side of the board on the ground and shift your weight over the roller. The goal is to keep the weight centered on top of the roller by shifting your weight left to right. (See the image on the left in Figure 7-1.) This tool is a great way to train your balance and reaction time, although keep in mind that its side-to-side rolling motion doesn't really mimic the motion of balancing on a SUP.

WARNING

Be careful when using a roller board because it can shoot out from under you and cause a hard fall. Start with someone stabilizing you or with holding onto something.

>> **Balancing with balance domes:** These balance trainers combine a soft, inflated ball with a hard surface. (See the center image in Figure 7-1.) Standing on the flat side is a good way to train your balance and is safer than a roller board (and a more realistic simulation of balancing on a

SUP). The level of balance challenge is relatively fixed, but you can adjust it slightly by changing the inflation pressure of the rubber dome.

>> **Rocking with rocker boards:** *Rocker boards* have curved rails or domes that do mimic the side-to-side rocking motion of a SUP more closely than roller boards do. They're also safer because a hard fall is less likely.

Many rocker boards have only one fixed curvature, which may be too easy — or too difficult — to balance on. At Blue Planet, we developed the Balance Surfer (shown on the right in Figure 7-1) as an adjustable balance training tool specifically for standup paddleboarding. It closely simulates the side-to-side balance on a SUP. The Balance Surfer comes with three balance modules that have two curvatures each and can be rotated by 90 degrees, resulting in seven different balance challenges from easy (think of it as a very long, wide, stable board) to extra challenging (a very narrow, tippy, low volume surf SUP board).

>> **Slacklining:** Balancing on a strap stretched between two trees or posts is a great way to train your balance and reflexes. It isn't a close simulation of the balance motion on a SUP, but it is another very challenging balance skill to master.

FIGURE 7-1: Roller board, balance dome, and rocker board.

Svitlana/Adobe Stock Photos   Adam Gregor/Adobe Stock Photos   ahavelaar/Adobe Stock Photos

Namaste

Yoga poses (for example, tree pose, where you balance on one foot) are especially helpful for balance training. The stretching, mindfulness, and intentional breathing of yoga are also excellent cross-training for paddlers; for more advanced yogis, doing the poses on a board is extra challenging and enjoyable. (For more on SUP yoga, check out Chapter 22.)

Cross-training

There are many ways to get and stay in shape and some of the cross training that will help you on the water includes strength training, cardiovascular training, stretching, and breathing exercises. More on each of these activities in this section.

REMEMBER

Before starting any new training programs, please consult with your doctor, start with easy/slow exercises, and don't overdo it.

Strength training

Though the balance exercises I mention in the earlier section "Working with balance trainers" do support leg and core strength and coordination, strength training can greatly improve paddle power, speed, and stamina.

REMEMBER

You don't have to go to a gym to do strength training. For years I've done my own five-minute morning exercise routine that incorporates stretches and body weight exercises, including push-ups and pull-ups.

TIP

Using weights at a gym can help build muscle mass if you increase the weights as you get stronger. Make sure to learn proper technique to avoid injury.

Cardio

Paddling for long distances takes endurance and stamina, so cardio cross-training is helpful. I like to go on challenging hikes, which combines both heart rate and balance training. *Interval training,* where you combine bursts of high intensity exercise with short breaks, is also very effective.

Stretching

Keeping your muscles limber by stretching regularly helps prevent injuries and makes paddling easier and more enjoyable. It's best to stretch when muscles are warmed up.

Breathing exercises

Without going into too much detail that's beyond the scope of this book, breathing plays a big role in paddling (and, you know, life). I regularly practice the following breathing exercises:

>> Box breathing:

   1. **Inhale for a count of four.**

   2. **Hold the air in your lungs for a count of four.**

   3. **Exhale for a count of four.**

   4. **Hold (with empty lungs) for a count of four.**

   5. **Repeat Steps 1 through 4.**

   When you think "box breathing," think "4 sides to a box." That will keep your count straight.

REMEMBER

>> Breathing meditation: Close your eyes and focus on breathing, counting each inhale and exhale. If your mind starts to wander, bring your focus back to your breath.

>> Wim Hof method breathing: The *Wim Hof* method involves quick, deep breaths followed by a breath hold. Here's an overview of how it works:

   1. **Sit or lie in a comfortable position.**

   2. **Take and release 30 deep breaths in succession.**

   3. **Take another breath and hold it until you feel like you need to breathe again.**

   4. **Take a big breath and hold it for 15 seconds, then release.**

   I've found this approach transformational. You can read more about the method at www.wimhofmethod.com/breathing-exercises. This YouTube video also does a great job of presenting it: youtu.be/tyb0i4hjZFQ?si=owe3p_dZLbR3d3E0

WARNING

   Don't do Wim Hof breathing in or near the water. Rarely, this method can lead people to lose consciousness.

>> **Timing breaths with strokes**: When I take paddle strokes, I time my breath with the stroke cadence. I inhale during the recovery phase and exhale during the power phase, taking one or two strokes per breath depending on the level of exertion. (For more on stroke cadences, flip to Chapter 11.)

STANDING UP, WALKING

Most people spend a lot of time sitting down — at work, driving or traveling, and while relaxing at home — often in poor ergonomic positions. For me, too much sitting has resulted in many health problems, including neck and back pain, poor posture, and low energy, all of which meant I had to make some adjustments to my lifestyle. Getting into SUP has benefitted me because I have to do it standing up (unlike kayaking, for example) and it engages my whole body.

But I can't paddle 24/7, so I also made some adjustments to my life-style and encourage you to do the same.

- I try to spend less time sitting down and avoiding poor posture like looking down at a phone or laptop screen.

- If I have to sit for long periods at work (like for writing this book), I use an adjustable sitting/standing desk that's more ergonomic. I regularly stand up and walk or stretch for a while before sitting back down.

- I avoid driving short distances to run errands and walk instead.

- When traveling on a plane or road trip, I make sure to regularly stand up to walk and stretch.

Chapter **8**

Before You Jump In

Y ou're probably eager to get out on the water, but before you jump in, you first have to

» Transport your gear to the water of your choosing, likely by vehicle

» Set up

» Check your equipment

» Make sure you understand the local rules and etiquette

» Have a safety plan in case things don't go as planned

I cover the transporting and rule-abiding steps in this chapter; head to Chapters 9 and 5 for more information on setup, equipment checks, and safety plans, respectively. Part 2 is where you can finally get your feet wet and start paddling.

Racking´ Em Up

If you're lucky, your equipment is already at the water's edge, and all you need to do is carry it a few feet to reach the water. Most people, though, first need to haul the gear to the beach (and then set it up, as I explain in Chapter 9). Most hard boards and inflated boards (iSUPs) are too big to fit inside a car or even a minivan, so in the following sections I go over some ways to transport boards by strapping them to a vehicle.

For more detailed tips for strapping boards to your vehicle, check out a YouTube video I made. You can find it at www.youtube.com/watch?v=TV-oCNLUCFg.

Going with sedans and SUVs

Properly securing your board to your vehicle is essential for safe transportation and to avoid damage to your board and car. Here's what needs to happen if you're rolling in a car or an SUV; pickup drivers, check out the following section:

1. **Gather your strapping equipment.**

   You need two cam buckle straps (one to two inches wide) to strap boards to a roof rack. If your vehicle doesn't have a rack, you can also use two rigid foam blocks to strap boards to your car.

   TIP

   I always opt for cam buckle straps over ratcheting straps because you're less likely to overtighten cams and damage your board. (Cam buckle straps rely just on your hand strength to make them secure. Ratcheting straps double down on the tension with the help of some — relatively simple — mechanics, which can be too much of a good thing.)

2. **Check your roof racks.**

   If your car has roof racks, make sure they're securely attached to the vehicle following the manufacturer's instructions. I recommend rack pads to protect your board.

   TIP

   If you plan to regularly transport your board, I highly suggest getting some good quality aftermarket roof racks fitted to your vehicle. And if you don't have roof racks, don't drive "naked": Definitely place foam blocks on your vehicle's roof to support your board.

3. **Load your board.**

   Place your board on the roof racks or foam blocks with the deck side down and fin pointing up. If you have a hard time lifting the board over your head, get someone to help you. If you're stacking two boards, put the longer board on first and have the fins pointing up and forward; then stagger the next board behind the fins of the first board, as Figure 8-1 shows.

4. **Secure the front end of the board.**

   Run the strap over the board, loop it around the roof rack and then back over the board, and strap it tightly.

   TIP

   If you don't have roof racks, you can open both front doors, run the strap through the inside of the car, and then loop it over the board (resting on your foam blocks) and tighten the strap.

   After you have the board strapped down securely, the board itself compresses and holds the foam blocks in place. This method isn't ideal; if you were to get some heavy rain, for example, water could very well leak into your car.

5. **Secure the back end of the board.**

   Repeat Step 4 with the rear strap, looping it around the back rack.

   If you don't have a rack, run the strap through the back doors of your car if your car has a four-door setup. If your car only has two doors, spread the straps out as far as possible with one strap at the front, and one at the back of the door opening.

6. **Test, adjust, and secure.**

Give the board a good tug to make sure it's secure and can't shift and loosen. Tighten the straps again if needed and tie off the ends of the straps. Always double-check everything before driving and monitor during transport.

TIP

When you tighten straps flat on top of the board, they tend to start vibrating and humming while you're driving. This movement results in a noisy ride and can damage the finish on your board. You can avoid this humming by simply leaving a twist in the strap so it doesn't lay flat on the board.

Safely strapping boards to a pickup truck

If you're transporting your SUP with a pickup truck, your best bet is to use a tailgate pad that provides both padding and a strap to secure the board. No tailgate pad? You can also use other padding to protect your board and secure the front of the board to the truck bed by using tie down straps.

Transporting inflatable boards

If you have an iSUP, you can usually carry it inside your vehicle, inflate it when you get to the water, deflate it after use, roll it up, and store it in its bag. If you regularly use your inflatable board, you may want to keep it inflated and transport it by strapping it to the roof of your vehicle as I explain in the preceding sections.

TIP

Leaving an iSUP inflated can prolong its useful life and save you the time and effort inflating, deflating, and packaging it takes. Just keep in mind that leaving an iSUP fully inflated for transport isn't a good idea because high temperatures can increase the pressure inside the board and could cause the seams to fail. If you do leave your iSUP inflated, you want to release some pressure before hauling it and then inflate it to full pressure before going into the water again.

If you are using a manual pump, take your time, make sure not to strain your back, and fully inflate the board to the recommended pressure. Inflatable boards have more flex than hard boards to start with and using an underinflated board can be a miserable experience. So take your time and make sure to pump up the board to the maximum recommended pressure.

REMEMBER

Using a good quality pump makes a big difference. Many pumps have two stages; the first stage quickly fills the board with air, and the second stage makes fully pressurizing the board easier. A good electric pump with a two-stage pump, rechargeable lithium battery, and automatic shutoff makes inflating the board much easier. Electric pumps can take a while, so set up and start the pump first and let it do its job while you change, apply sunscreen, and get everything else ready.

TIP

Note that the gauge on your manual pump may not show a pressure reading even when the board appears to be full of air. Keep pumping and the needle on the gauge should start to move once there is over 1-2 psi of pressure.

Being a Good Neighbor at Your Local Beach

As a stand up paddleboarder, you share the water with not only other paddlers but also swimmers, surfers, boaters, and other beachgoers. Being a good neighbor is essential for ensuring everyone's safety and enjoyment. It fosters a positive community and protects the natural beauty of your beloved waterways for all to enjoy.

In this section, I go over the key aspects of being considerate and responsible, including access rules, local laws, and good SUP etiquette.

Knowing the local access rules

Before you hit the water, familiarize yourself with access rules at your local waterway. These rules help manage the use of the beach and water.

>> **Know the designated areas.** Many beaches have defined areas for different activities. Look for signs indicating where paddleboarding, swimming, surfing, and boating are allowed. Respect these zones to avoid conflict and accidents, and always make sure to avoid swimmers.

>> **Use designated launch areas.** Some waterways have specific launch and landing areas for SUPs. Using these areas helps prevent congestion and accidents, especially at busy beaches.

>> **Respect private property.** Avoid launching from private property without permission; stick to public access points to make sure you aren't trespassing. Some marinas and inland waterways may also be considered private property and not open to public use.

>> **Obey parking regulations.** Park in dedicated areas and avoid blocking driveways and access points. Pay attention to whether parking fees or permits are required.

Respecting local laws

Understanding and adhering to local regulations keeps you out of trouble. These laws vary by location, so make sure you're up-to-date on your destination's rules on the following before you paddle out:

>> **Licensing and permits:** Some areas may require permits or licenses for paddling. Check with local authorities or beach management for any necessary paperwork.

>> **Safety gear:** Local authorities may mandate the use of specific safety gear, such as personal floatation devices (PFDs), signaling devices, and leashes. Ensure you have the required gear and know how to use it. You can read more about these safety items in Chapter 5.

>> **Right of way:** Know the laws governing right of way for waterways. Avoid boat channels and busy waterways, even if you have the right of way.

As I explain in the following section, swimmers always have the right of way over SUPs.

REMEMBER

>> **Environmental protection:** Be aware of laws aimed at protecting local wildlife and natural habitats. Avoid approaching or disturbing wildlife, and don't enter protected areas. Leave no trace by packing out trash and minimizing your impact.

Practicing SUP etiquette

Good etiquette on and off the water ensures a pleasant experience for all. Help create a friendly, respectful, helpful, and safe environment by following these guidelines:

>> **Respect other water users.** Be courteous to other paddlers, swimmers, surfers, and boaters. Give them ample space and avoid interfering with their activities.

>> **Stay out of the surf zone.** If you aren't surfing, stay clear of the surf zone. Breaking waves can be dangerous, and your board can endanger others. (If you feel ready to surf, check out Chapter 13, where I cover SUP surfing etiquette.)

>> **Yield to swimmers.** Always give right of way to swimmers; they often can't see you coming and may not always swim in a straight line. Avoid paddling close to crowded swimming areas.

>> **Avoid making a racket.** Keep the noise levels down, especially in areas where people are relaxing and enjoying nature. Some people enjoy using a waterproof speaker to listen to music while paddling, but don't assume the people around you also enjoy listening to your music.

>> **Help others in need.** If you see someone in trouble, always offer assistance if it's safe to do so. Be prepared to call for help if needed.

>> **Use the buddy system.** As I say in Chapter 5, paddling with others is more fun and safer.

REMEMBER

If you do go by yourself, share a float plan with someone on shore, follow safety protocol, and don't take unnecessary risks.

>> **Clean up after yourself (and maybe others).** Don't be a litterbug. I like to leave the beach and water cleaner than I found it. If I see plastic or trash in the water or on the beach, I stop to pick it up and dispose of it at the nearest trash can. Try to make this good deed a habit; it feels good.

Being a good neighbor not only fosters a positive community but also protects the natural beauty of our beloved waterways for all to enjoy.

Get Up, Stand Up

Get the hang of balancing and paddling on your board.

Recognize and steer clear of common beginner mistakes.

Chapter **9**

Stand Up Comedy: Your First Balancing Act

At the Blue Planet Adventure rental operation in Hale'iwa (and at our free SUP Clinics) our business has introduced thousands of people to stand up paddleboarding. It can be quite entertaining (dare I say "hilarious"?) to watch people stand up for the first time and struggle with balancing on the water while using a paddle to propel themselves forward. You may get a taste of humble pie on your first attempts, but don't worry. My fellow instructors and I all started out as beginners, so we all know what it's like. And, to make the early days easier for you, I have put together some helpful tips for getting started.

In this chapter you will finally get your feet wet! Think of it as your first balancing act, and like any good comedy, it's all about timing, practice, and having fun. Even if you are already an experienced paddler you may find some helpful tips in this chapter and if anything, it will make you a better instructor when you teach others how to do it.

Watch Your Back: Set Up, Lifting, and Carrying Your Gear Like a Pro

Setting up and carrying your gear to the shoreline properly before you hit the water is crucial. The following sections offer a step-by-step guide to get you started.

Attaching the fin

If your board doesn't have a fin attached yet, do that now. On many inflatable boards, you slide the fin into the slot and secure it with a clip. On most hard boards, you slide the fin into the fin box, line up the screw hole with the fin plate in the box, and then secure the fin with the screw. (Make sure to bring the needed tools to do this job.) You can read more about fins and so on in Chapter 2; Chapter 3 is where I cover inflatable and hard boards.

Connecting the leash

No ifs, ands, or buts here: Always use a leash, no matter what. As Chapter 5 explains, a leash is the only thing keeping the board from getting away from you if you fall — and you *will* fall, probably more than once. When that happens, reaching down to your ankle cuff and pulling the board toward you using the leash is often easier than swimming toward the board.

The leash usually comes with a leash line that loops around the leash plug on the tail of the board. You then securely attach the *rail saver* (the straps that connect the leash to the leash string on the board, as shown in Figure 5-1) over the line, making sure to fully open the closure. The other end of the leash then attaches around your ankle.

REMEMBER

Make sure the closure is lined up properly and the leash fits snugly, but not too tightly, around your ankle. A good leash is crucial for safety; check for frayed lines and worn-out closure material and replace your leash every five years or so as the urethane material deteriorates over time.

Using a personal floatation device (PFD)

In most locations, the same rules for boating apply to paddle-boarders. That usually means you're required to have a personal floatation device. Make sure that yours fits well and that you properly adjust the buckles and straps.

WARNING

You should always wear a PFD. Typically, the rules require only that you have it attached to your board, but that approach defeats the whole purpose of the PFD and gives you a false sense of security. In an emergency, you'll have to be able to get back to your board for the PFD to help you. And if you can make it back to your board (itself a big floatation device), you no longer need a PFD anyway.

Flip to Chapter 5 for more info on the various types of PFDs.

Carrying your board

Don't try to use the handle to lift the board flat off the ground (or off the water). First, lift the rail of the board to stand the board on its side with the handle facing away from you; then grab the handle and lift the board up, using your legs and keeping your back straight.

TIP

If you have to go over a wall or use stairs, you may want to carry the board over your shoulder to prevent damage to the rail.

Putting your board in the water

The easiest place to launch a paddleboard is a gently sloping beach. Just make sure you carry the board into knee-deep water before setting it down so the fin doesn't get stuck in the sand or mud.

Going from Kneeling to Standing Tall

Learning to balance on a SUP is akin to mastering the first act of your stand up comedy routine — once you've nailed balancing on a SUP, everything else becomes easier. (Everything SUP related, anyway.) Sometimes, though, getting the hang of balance is a tall order. That's why I break down the process in the following sections.

Starting on your knees

Position yourself on the center of the board. Place your knees on either side of the carry handle as shown on the left in Figure 9-1 and center your weight over the center line of the board. Stay on your knees at first because keeping your center of gravity lower helps you find stability before attempting to stand up in deeper water.

FIGURE 9-1: Mounting your board and practicing strokes.

Taking some practice strokes

In the kneeling position, take some paddle strokes to get a feel for how to propel and steer the board using your paddle. Hold the paddle lower on the shaft when in a kneeling position as the center image in Figure 9-1 illustrates; your top hand doesn't have to reach the handle at the top of the shaft while kneeling. Paddle on both sides, making sure to switch your hands on the paddle every time you switch sides. A couple of other things to try:

>> Steering the board

>> Putting the paddle behind you and paddling backward as shown on the right in Figure 9-1 to experience how doing so turns your board

Before you actually try to stand up, be sure to paddle into deeper water and away from any hard objects such as docks, rocks, or posts in the water. If you fall close to hard objects, you risk hitting your head or other body parts. If you fall in shallow water, you risk cutting your feet on sharp objects on the bottom, and could hurt your knees, ankles, or wrists, when hitting the bottom.

If you're struggling with balance in the kneeling position, you aren't ready to stand up. And that's okay. Just keep paddling in a kneeling or sitting position until you get comfortable, and then try to stand up. You may also want to consider finding calmer conditions; using a wider, more stable board; or practicing your balance with a balance board.

Standing up

Some people just keep paddling in a kneeling or sitting position as it's easier to balance and that's fine, but the whole point of stand up paddleboarding is to paddle in a standing position, otherwise you might as well just use a kayak that's designed for paddling comfortably in a sitting position. So, once you feel stable and comfortable in the kneeling position, it's time to stand up and find your "sea legs."

Here's how it works:

1. **Place your paddle across the board in front of your knees, keeping your hands on the paddle.**

2. **Slowly rise and put your feet where your knees were, on either side of the center carry handle.**

   The image on the left in Figure 9-2 shows a paddler partway through this step.

3. **Place your feet parallel, pointing forward, about shoulder width apart or a bit wider.**

4. **Lift up your paddle as you stand up and put the blade in the water as shown on the right in Figure 9-2.**

   Doing so gives you added stability; think of your paddle as a walking stick.

FIGURE 9-2:
Moving from kneeling to standing.

Finding your sea legs on a tippy log

After you're actually standing (see the preceding section), main-taining balance is crucial — and not as easy as it looks. The following sections offer some balance tips to help you find your sea legs.

Focus forward

If you look down at your feet, paddle, board, or the water, that's where you end up going. Stand up straight and look forward at the horizon or something stable on land, and don't think too much about how to balance. This strategy helps shift your focus to where you want to go and lets your legs do the balancing.

TECHNICAL STUFF

The fine adjustments needed to maintain your balance come from your *somatic nervous system*; the brain is often too slow to consciously give the commands, so your body relies on reflexes.

TIP

Try not to look at your feet and think about how to balance as you are likely to react too slowly and/or overreact. It's best to just look forward, relax, and let your legs do the job.

Body position

The best body position for SUP is the one shown on the left in Figure 9-3: Keep your knees slightly bent, your core engaged, your upper body upright (not hunched over), and your paddle in the water for balance. This way, your legs and core can absorb the small side-to-side balancing movements necessary to keep you from making a splash landing — which is what the poor-posture paddler on the right in Figure 9-3 is likely headed for.

FIGURE 9-3:
Comparing
good and
bad body
position.

Weight distribution

Make sure your feet are symmetrical on the board (same distance from the center line) so your weight is distributed evenly between both feet. Also make sure you aren't too far forward or too far back on the board, because this placement creates more drag and makes the board less stable.

Use the board's center handle as an orientation point when determining foot placement.

TIP

Keeping Your Board on the Straight and Narrow

Effective paddling strokes keep your board moving forward in a straight line. Use forward strokes and switch the paddle to the other side of the board every few strokes to keep the board going straight. Use steering strokes to turn the board.

Forward strokes

To do an efficient forward stroke, reach forward and insert the paddle blade fully into the water with the paddle shaft perpendicular to the water. Then pull it back in a straight line close to the board.

The most effective part of the stroke happens in front of your feet, so pull until the paddle reaches your feet. Then take it out of the water and bring it forward for the next stroke. The more effective your forward strokes become, the less often you need to switch sides to go keep going straight.

Steering stroke

Turning your paddleboard is key to navigating. Enter the steering stroke. Also known as a *sweep stroke*, the *steering stroke* makes the board turn more quickly, giving you a wide turn while keeping your forward momentum.

REMEMBER

Extend the paddle away from the board at a diagonal angle and make a wide arc from the front to the back. To turn left, paddle on the right side; to turn right, paddle on the left side.

Reverse stroke

To slow down and turn more quickly — when trying to avoid an obstacle, for example — perform the steering stroke in the opposite direction (reverse sweep stroke). That means putting the paddle into the water behind your feet and pushing the blade forward. This stroke slows you down and turns the board toward the side you're taking the reverse stroke on.

Taking a Fall and Getting Right Back Onboard

Falling off your board is part of the learning process. At some point, you'll definitely lose your balance and fall in the water. Be prepared for getting wet by dressing for the occasion (see Chapter 6 for more on that topic) and try to remain calm. The following sections help you fall as gracefully — or at least safely — as possible and get back to paddling.

Falling without hurting yourself

If you lose your balance, you may instinctively try to catch yourself by falling on your board, but do your best to avoid this common mistake.

WARNING

Falling onto the board is the most common way beginners get hurt. They end up (potentially) hurting their knees, hips, wrist, arms, and shoulders and, if they're especially unlucky, damaging their boards as well.

So when you lose your balance, try to fall into the water; it's soft and won't hurt you, unlike the board. Also try to fall flat into the water (like a starfish) so you don't go too deep into the water. If you jump feet-first into shallow water, you can hit the bottom and hurt yourself.

Re-boarding and regaining your balance

When you fall off, your board can get away from you quickly, that's why it's important to always wear a leash. When you fall into the water, it's often easier to reach down to your ankle cuff and pull the board towards you using the leash, rather than swimming towards the board.

To get back on your board after a fall, position yourself next to the board and grab the center handle or the far side of the board. Kick your legs behind you, like you're swimming, to get them close to the water surface and then slide your chest onto the deck of the board. If you've lost your paddle, you can use your arms to *prone-paddle* the board (like you would a surfboard) to go retrieve the paddle.

TIP

People who struggle to get back on the board are usually kicking with their feet down under the board, like they're trying to push off the bottom. Pulling yourself up onto the board while kicking downward is almost impossible, so make sure you kick your feet behind you, get your body close to the surface, and then slide your chest onto the deck of the board while kicking with your feet behind you.

After your chest is back on the board, you can swing your legs back around so you're facing the nose of the board. Then get back into the kneeling position I cover earlier in the chapter with your knees on either side of the center handle. Take your time, take some deep breaths, and find your balance while doing some strokes on your knees before standing up.

REMEMBER

The board is more stable when it moves forward, so getting some momentum going while paddling on your knees — before you try to stand up again — is helpful.

Don't Forget to Have Fun!

Mastering the basics of SUP is like delivering your first comedy routine: It requires practice, patience, and a willingness to laugh at yourself. With the basic skills covered in this chapter you're well on your way to enjoying the unique and rewarding experience of "walking on water." So, stay humble, get out there, embrace the wobble, keep paddling, and most importantly, don't forget to have fun on the water!

IN THIS CHAPTER

» Holding the paddle correctly

» Putting that paddle to good use

» Finding the perfect trim

» Riding in a way that doesn't batter your board

Chapter **10**

Avoiding the Most Common Rookie Mistakes

R ight off the bat, let me tell you that I've watched many first-time paddlers make the same simple mistakes repeatedly. If you can just avoid the common issues I outline in this chapter, you're well ahead of the average beginner.

Before giving first time paddlers instructions, I make sure to ask them first if they would like some tips. Some don't, but most beginners appreciate a few helpful tips if given in an encouraging way. I have heard a golfer say that practice does not make perfect, practice makes permanent, so I always encourage people to learn good technique early on as it can be hard to "unlearn" bad technique once it becomes a habit. In this chapter, I will go over some of the most common mistakes and how to avoid them.

Looking at Paddle Handling Pitfalls

You may think I'm focusing too much on the negative and betraying the Hawaiian *shaka* ("hang loose") attitude in the process but trust me: Figuring out what *not* to do is just as important as figuring out what *to* do. Hopefully the following sections make that clear.

TIP

When you're able to recognize common errors, you may find you want to offer well-intentioned help to newbie paddlers making those mistakes. Don't jump straight into instruction mode, though. Most beginners appreciate a few helpful suggestions — given in an encouraging way — but some don't. Before giving first-time paddlers instructions, I make sure to ask them first whether they want some tips.

Holding the paddle blade backward

As I discuss in Chapter 4, most paddles have a *canter* or angle between the shaft and the blade designed to keep the blade vertical to the water for as long as possible during the stroke. Many beginners (including me when I first started) tend to hold the blade backward, intuitively thinking that the blade will scoop more water if it's angled toward them as shown on the left in Figure 10-1. Experienced paddlers cringe when they see newbies with the blade held backwards but before you offer others well-intentioned help, I recommend asking first to make sure that tips are welcome.

REMEMBER

The correct way to hold the paddle is with the blade angled forward, away from you, as shown in the center image in Figure 10-1. This angle creates lift at the beginning of the stroke and keeps the blade perpendicular to the water for longer, propelling you forward and minimizing drag. (See the image on the right in Figure 10-1.)

FIGURE 10-1:
Incorrect
and correct
paddle
holding
position.

If you hold paddle with the blade backward, angled toward you, it has a negative angle to the water through most of the stroke, creating a downward force that compresses the board onto the water and slows you down.

Not switching hands on the shaft

Neglecting to switch your hands on the shaft when switching sides with the paddle results in an awkward body position, which you can see on the left in Figure 10-2. When switching the paddle from one side of the board to the other, your hands should also switch (see the center image in Figure 10-2) so the bottom hand is on the outside. (The image on the right in Figure 10-2 shows proper hand placement.)

FIGURE 10-2:
Switching
hands
versus not
switching
hands.

Not paying attention to grip distance

Beginners often tend to hold their hands too close together on the paddle, which results in poor leverage on the paddle and makes propelling yourself forward cumbersome. A wider grip improves leverage and increases the power you can apply to the paddle.

TIP

A good way to measure grip distance is by using the *paddlers box* technique shown in Figure 10-3. Place the paddle on top of your head with one hand on the handle and adjust the hand on the shaft so your elbows are at roughly right angles.

FIGURE 10-3: Using the paddlers box to determine a good grip distance.

Steering Clear of Board Handling Blunders

Like most things in life, there's more than one way to mess up in stand up paddleboarding. I walk you through some paddle-related errors in the earlier section "Looking at Paddle Handling Pitfalls"; in this section, I tackle board handling mistakes.

Not balancing your weight at the center of the board

REMEMBER

The board glides best and is most stable when the flat section on the bottom of the board is parallel to the water (as in Figure 10-4b). That means putting your feet — and therefore your weight — in the center of the board.

If your feet are too far back on the board (as shown in Figure 10-4a), the tail sinks, making the board less stable and creating more drag. If your feet are too far forward on the board (as shown in Figure 10-4c), the tail sticks out of the water and the nose rocker creates more drag by pushing water in the front.

On most boards, putting your feet on either side of the center handle results in a good *trim position* — the foot position where the board glides smoothly with minimal drag.

Coming in hot: Trying to dismount too quickly/from standing

A common and potentially dangerous mistake is being too gung-ho on the dismount. Some paddlers come toward the beach at full speed in a standing position. When the board hits the bottom, it stops suddenly, and the paddler falls forward or jumps off feet first. This kind of approach can not only cause injury but also damage the board.

The better way to land is to slow down, get back down on your knees, and step off carefully with one foot as Figure 10-5 illustrates. Basically, you're doing the reverse of getting up on the board (flip to Chapter 9 for more on that process).

Before you walk away from your board, make sure to remove the *leash* attaching you to it. I've seen people get tripped up by the leash and almost face-plant.

Not lifting up the board correctly at the end of the day

Whether you're pulling the board off the ground or off the water surface, lift up the rail with one hand first before lifting up the board using the center handle. You can see this method in Figure 10-6. When the board is flat in the water, the suction created by the water's surface tension makes lifting the board straight up very difficult. Don't force it and hurt your back.

Not keeping your goal in mind

As I mention in Chapter 9, the key to stand up paddleboard success is making sure you're always looking forward and that you just go for it and start paddling until you find your balance. Many beginners make the mistake of a) looking down and b) overthinking it, which usually leads to their losing their balance and ending up in the drink.

Not paddling upwind first

WARNING

Beginners often don't realize that the wind or a current is what's pushing them along. When they finally try to turn around and go back to the starting point, fighting that outside force can be a real struggle. It can also be dangerous in strong offshore wind conditions, where beginners often have to be rescued because they just can't make it back on their own.

So before you go in, assess the wind and current. If in doubt, don't go out. If the wind and current are light, paddle upwind (or up-current) first, as Figure 10-7 demonstrates, so the return trip is easier. I suggest some tools for checking wind, current, and other conditions in Chapter 7. Tips for paddling into the wind are covered in Chapter 11.

FIGURE 10-7:
Paddling into the wind first so coming back is easy.

3

Leveling Up: From Wobbly Novice to Zen Waterman

IN THIS PART . . .

Familiarize yourself with the stroke phases and some more advanced paddle maneuvers.

Unleash your competitive spirit with SUP racing.

Hang ten as you discover SUP surfing.

Chapter **11**

So You're No Longer a Beginner . . .

When I coach entry-level paddlers, I try to teach good paddle technique as soon as possible as it's easy for beginners to pick up efficient technique quickly. I find it's often more difficult for experienced paddlers to change their habits if they have been paddling with poor technique for a long time. So ideally, once you have mastered the basics covered in Part 2, you are ready to learn some more advanced stroke technique that will make you a more efficient paddler.

Stroke of Genius: Mastering Efficient Paddle Technique

Paddle strokes are all about efficiency because a good stroke technique lets you conserve energy, go faster, paddle longer distances, and control your direction. In the following sections, I break down the basic components of an efficient paddle stroke.

Phases of the stroke: C.P.E.R

Just think "CPR" with an added *E* in the middle: CPER — catch, power phase, exit, recovery.

The Catch

The *catch* is where the paddle first enters the water — and just so you know, every efficient stroke starts with a good catch. Reach forward as far as you comfortably can; aim for a clean, splash-free entry; and bury the whole blade in the water before you start the power phase. (See the following section.)

If you start pulling on the paddle too early, before you get a good catch, you pull air bubbles down into the water. These bubbles make your paddle slip through the water rather than get good traction. The idea is to firmly plant the blade into the water and then pull yourself toward and past the blade. You aren't pulling the paddle through the water; you're pulling yourself forward toward the planted blade.

TIP

Think of planting your blade firmly into the water, like you're sticking it into thick chocolate pudding.

The Power phase

The *power phase* is where you propel the board forward. You can apply power in many ways, and every paddler has their unique style.

REMEMBER

You want to set up the power phase with a solid catch, as I explain in the preceding section.

I like to break the power phase into three ingredients that you can combine to create a more powerful stroke:

1. Lean.

Load up the paddle by leaning forward, pushing down with your top hand, and using gravity to "fall" onto the paddle. Avoid relying on your arms to do all the work; keep them fairly straight and apply power by engaging your stronger core, torso, lats, and back muscles. Toward the end of your stroke, bring your hips back forward and straighten your back as you exit the blade. (Check out the following section for more on the exit.)

2. **Twist.**

   Rotate your hips and shoulders forward toward your bottom hand on the shaft; this move extends your reach farther forward. After a clean catch, with your blade fully planted into the water, unwind the twist by squaring your hips and shoulders.

TIP

   Think of your body as a coiled-up spring that you load up as you twist, and then release that tension into your power phase by releasing your hips and shoulders.

3. **Stack your shoulders.**

   To drive the board straight forward (instead of turning it), you want to pull the blade straight back with the shaft vertical to the water. For the paddle to be vertical, your top hand must be directly above your bottom hand, which means you need to stack your top shoulder over your bottom shoulder, reaching your top hand out over the opposite rail. To stay balanced on the board, you push your hips out to the opposite side.

Figure 11-1 shows the power phase; as you look at it, note the following:

>> The shaft position is vertical, with my top hand directly over my bottom hand and my stacked shoulders and hips balancing out, keeping the body weight over the center of the board.

>> The blade is fully planted in the water and close to the rail while I lean into the stroke and drive the paddle down with my top hand.

>> My arms are almost straight, and the power comes from my stronger core, lats, and back muscles.

After your feet reach the paddle, the blade angle quickly turns *negative* (you're pulling water up rather than propelling yourself forward), so the stroke becomes much less effective as it passes your feet. Therefore, the goal is to end the power phase as soon as the blade reaches your feet and to have the blade quickly exit the water smoothly and without splashing.

FIGURE 11-1:
Power
phase.

REMEMBER

Beginners often have the misconception that long strokes must be more effective, and they often pull on the paddle until they throw water up into the air behind themselves at the end of the stroke. Lifting water upward is a complete waste of energy; it isn't propelling you forward and can actually slow you down by compressing the board into the water. Instead, practice taking shorter, quicker forward strokes without pulling past your feet. Your strokes will become more efficient, resulting in more speed with less effort.

The Exit

How do you ensure a smooth exit? The key here is *feathering* the blade by twisting its power face (the side of the blade compressing the water, see Chapter 4) outward as soon as the power phase ends. (Head to the preceding section for details on the power phase.) Think of feathering as turning a doorknob with your top hand, pointing your thumb forward as you twist.

Feathering the blade allows the blade to start moving forward even before it fully exits the water; if you time it right, it propels the blade forward into the recovery (outlined in the following section). Feathering also allows you to bring the paddle very close to the rail at the end of your stroke without touching the rail with the blade as you lift it up.

TIP
Feathering is essential to a clean exit and recovery, so try to get a handle on it as soon as possible. I've found that paddlers who've paddled for a long time without feathering have a very difficult time with it because they must unlearn the muscle memory they've developed from many hours of paddling without it.

Focus on the following as you look at the photo in Figure 11-2:

>> I feather the paddle during exit, with the power face twisted out, away from the board.

>> The paddle exits close to my feet.

FIGURE 11-2: Exit and recovery.

The Recovery

The *recovery* gives you a moment to relax your muscles, straighten your back, and inhale as you prepare for the next catch and power phase (which I cover earlier in the chapter). The board decelerates while you're bringing the paddle back forward to prepare for the next stroke, so you want to keep the recovery as quick as possible, spending more time accelerating the board forward instead.

TIP

Keep the blade in the feathered position as you recover; doing so means you have less drag, especially when paddling into the wind. Bring the blade angle back to square to the water just before the next catch. You also want to keep the blade close to the water during this stage and avoid making a big, inefficient circular motion with the paddle as you recover. This technique also allows you to quickly brace with the paddle if you lose your balance.

Look at Figure 11-2 in the preceding section and note the following about the recovery:

>> The blade stays close to the water.

>> My hips are forward and my upper body straight and relaxed.

>> The recovery is a good time to inhale.

Forward Strokes: Keeping It on the Straight and Narrow

Understanding the difference between a forward stroke and a steering stroke is essential for maneuvering your board. When you want to go forward, you use a forward stroke as I describe in the earlier section "Stroke of Genius: Mastering the Phases of the Forward Stroke." If you're having trouble keeping the board going in a straight line and can only take one or two strokes before having to switch sides, here are some tips to help you take more strokes per side by propelling yourself forward rather than sideways. You can see them in action in Figure 11-3:

>> **Vertical paddle position:** Getting the paddle in a vertical position (refer to Figure 11-1 earlier in the chapter) is key to propelling yourself forward. Holding the paddle diagonally across your body makes the board turn.

TIP

Make a window with your arms and paddle and look forward through the window to make sure your paddle is vertical and your top hand is out over the rail.

>> **Stroke path:** Don't follow the outline of your board; instead, plant the blade slightly away from the rail and pull it straight back or slightly toward you, ending with the shaft right next to the rail as it reaches your feet.

>> **Blade angle:** If the blade is angled outward, away from the board, the stroke turns the board. Instead, angle the blade slightly inward, pulling the water toward you.

FIGURE 11-3:
Hacks for propelling your board forward.

TIP

You can paddle on one side indefinitely by using *reverse J strokes.* To do this stroke, you plant the paddle farther away from the rail and pull the blade toward you in a reverse letter *J* as shown in Figure 11-4. Notice that the blade is angled toward me and the stroke path curves toward me.

FIGURE 11-4:
Reverse J stroke path.

Surveying Steering Strokes and Maneuvers

If you want your board to turn, you basically do the opposite of a forward stroke. That means making like the paddler in Figure 11-5: getting the paddle out as far away from the board as possible; holding the shaft diagonally and with your top hand lower to the water; making a wide, sweeping, curved stroke called a *sweep stroke* in the water, with the paddle blade angled out; and pushing the paddle out and far away from the rail at the beginning of the stroke.

FIGURE 11-5: Steering stroke.

Turning on a dime: Rotating faster

If sweep strokes aren't turning you fast enough, like when you need to avoid an obstacle, try one of the following:

>> **Reverse sweep stroke:** Use a *reverse sweep stroke* by placing the paddle behind you and pushing it forward. This technique slows you down and turns the board quickly to the side you're paddling backward on. After the board starts to move backward, however, reverse strokes are less effective and the board becomes more tippy. If you start moving backward and want to keep turning, switch the paddle to the other side and take forward steering strokes on the opposite side.

>> **Cross-bow turn:** The *cross-bow turn* is another quick way to turn without losing as much forward momentum as with a reverse sweep stroke. You steer by reaching the paddle over the bow of the board (keeping your hands in the same position), angling the blade toward the rail, and pulling the blade toward the bow to adjust course, as shown in Figure 11-6.

FIGURE 11-6:
Cross-bow
turn.

>> **Pivot turn:** A faster (and more challenging) way to turn is the *pivot turn,* shown in Figure 11-7, where you move your weight back to sink the tail. Doing so allows the board to pivot quickly when you're using steering strokes. The pivot turn is a good move to have in your repertoire when you want to pivot quickly to catch a wave coming toward you. Paddlers often use this turn in SUP racing because it allows tight turns around buoys, even on long race boards.

Practicing pivot turns is a great way to prepare for SUP surfing because it requires you to switch from a *parallel stance* (where you have your feet on either side of the board with your toes pointing forward) to a *surf stance* (where your feet are on the center line of the board with one foot forward and one foot back). The board becomes less stable after the tail sinks, and balancing side to side in surf stance is trickier.

TIP

FIGURE 11-7:
Pivot turn.

REMEMBER

The advantage of being in surf stance is that you can quickly move your weight from nose to tail by shifting it between your front and back foot or shuffling your feet back and forth along the center line of the board without rocking the board side to side. Moving your weight from front to back in surf stance while bracing with your paddle is another good way to practice your balance ability before attempting to SUP surf in the waves (see Chapter 13) or paddling downwind in rough conditions (see the following section).

For more tips on these turns, check out these two YouTube videos I put together:

>> **Cross-bow turn:** www.youtube.com/watch?v=00As8-AMe6g

>> **Pivot turn:** www.youtube.com/watch?v=jIpkzGDrT9k

Paddling upwind and in currents

As I explain in Chapter 7, beginner paddlers should avoid windy conditions and currents. As you get better, though, you can start to challenge yourself in more difficult conditions. (But don't overdo it!)

On a windy day, paddling straight into the wind is easier than paddling sideways to it. Just keep your nose pointed straight into the wind and switch sides whenever you start to veer off course in either direction. The more you veer off, the more difficult turning back into the wind becomes, so try to keep the nose pointed straight into the wind.

If you can set your own course on a windy day, plan to paddle straight upwind, if possible, and then come back straight downwind. If you must go across the wind to reach your destination, you won't be able to reach it by pointing your nose straight toward your goal because the wind will blow you far downwind of where you intended to go. Instead, you have to *ferry* across like you would a river. That means pointing your nose into the wind (or current) at a slight angle and paddling into the wind (or current) as you move sideways. The stronger the wind or current, the steeper you must point your nose into it.

If you're paddling into a crosswind, you may have to take hard steering strokes with every stroke just to keep the board going straight.

Standing up, you have more surface area catching the wind, so kneeling or sitting down on the board may help reduce the wind resistance if you're struggling. You can even lay the paddle blade under your chest and paddle in a prone position with your arms like you'd paddle a surfboard for the least wind resistance.

In strong gusts, you can lower your wind resistance in a standing position by lowering your grip on the paddle and bending your knees into a crouch. Feathering the blade, keeping the recovery quick, and keeping the paddle in the water as much as possible also helps when you're paddling into a strong headwind. I cover these topics in the earlier section "Stroke of Genius: Mastering the Phases of the Forward Stroke."

Paddling into the wind is challenging because you can exhaust yourself just paddling in place — you can even move backwards if you are not paddling hard enough to overcome the pressure of the wind pushing against you. That's why going out in offshore winds is so dangerous for beginners. Always check the conditions and weather forecast (flip to Chapter 7 for my tips on that step) and paddle upwind first. And above all, if in doubt, don't go out.

Chapter **12**

The Need for Speed: Getting into SUP Racing and Endurance Paddling

A fter I figured out the basics of SUP, all I wanted to do was surf waves. One day, though, when the surf was small and the lineup was crowded, I started to paddle along the coast to see how far I could go and found it very enjoyable. I ended up paddling for several miles and got hooked on paddling longer distances. I soon made friends with other distance paddlers, and we went on long training paddles together, which led to my entering my first SUP race back in 2008.

I soon set a goal of completing one of the most challenging races in the world, the 32-mile Molokai to Oahu (M2O) Paddleboard World Championships. I have since completed it more than ten times. The last few miles of the M2O race, such as the bit in Figure 12-1, are especially rough and mentally challenging.

FIGURE 12-1:
Rounding
Portlock
Point on the
way to the
M2O race
finish.

SUP training and racing has been a great way for me to improve my technique and to get (and stay) in shape, both physically and mentally. SUP racing is a dynamic and rewarding sport that challenges you to push your physical and mental limits in a supportive community of fellow enthusiasts. Whether you're competing for the thrill, the camaraderie, or the personal challenge, SUP racing has something to offer everyone. So grab your paddle, hit the water, and experience the joys of SUP racing for yourself!

Discovering the Joy of Distance Paddling

Whether you are training competitively or just out for a leisurely paddle, gliding smoothly over the water and covering long distances powered only by your paddle is an exhilarating experience. Long-distance paddling and racing offer a unique blend of physical endurance and strength, technique, mental focus, plugging into nature, and the community spirit that comes from sharing the fun with other paddlers.

The thrill of speed

One of the most exciting aspects of paddling on a fast board is the sheer speed you can achieve. As you refine your technique and build your strength, you find yourself gliding across the water with increasing swiftness and less effort. The feeling of flying over the water, powered by your own strength and skill, is incredibly satisfying — and can be addictive!

Endurance and stamina

REMEMBER

Training for and competing in long-distance races emphasizes endurance. Paddling at high speed for a few minutes is easy, but doing so over many miles is a test of physical stamina and mental fortitude. The physical conditioning and mental resilience required to complete a long training paddle or a grueling race is unparalleled and creates a great sense of accomplishment.

Coming Up with Your Own Training Program

If you want to become a faster, stronger paddler, you need to commit to a structured training program. Having a training plan can lead to faster improvements and better results. Although you can train on your own for fun, competing in races and training with other fast paddlers can motivate you to work and push you to try harder than you would paddling by yourself.

The type of race you're preparing for plays a role in your training plan. Clearly, you want to prepare yourself to perform in the type of conditions and distance expected on race day.

REMEMBER

I cover cross-training later in the chapter.

Perceived effort

Perceived effort is a percentage of your maximum effort, which correlates to heart rate. When you sprint and paddle as hard as you possibly can for about 60 seconds, that's 100 percent effort.

TECHNICAL STUFF

When you sprint at 100 percent effort, your muscles consume more oxygen than your blood can supply. This pace is *anaerobic*, and the human body can't maintain it over longer periods.

Over longer distances, the goal is to maintain a pace at around 80 percent of your maximum. If you can improve your top sprint speed (your 100 percent effort number) by 10 percent, your 80 percent effort number will likely experience the same boost.

REMEMBER

Maintaining good technique at 100 percent effort is more challenging than doing so at a slower pace, and you train your heart rate to recover quickly when you slow down the pace. As a result, opting for a sprint pace followed by a recovery phase is an excellent way to improve conditioning and technique, even if you're training for long-distance racing.

Interval training

A training plan should include some days where you focus on *interval training*, alternating between high-intensity sprints and moderately paced recovery. This approach is very effective at improving performance without doing a long paddle. The goal is to push yourself as hard as possible over short sprints, bringing your heart rate close to the maximum rate.

A typical interval training session may look like this:

1. Warm up for five minutes at approximately 60 percent effort.
2. Sprint for one minute at 100 percent effort.
3. Recover for two minutes at 60 percent effort.
4. Repeat Steps 2 and 3 three to six times.
5. Cool down for five minutes at 60 percent effort.

A good training program combines two or three days per week of interval training days, where you focus on speed and technique, combined with one or two long paddle days per week where you focus on conditioning, stamina, and endurance. You can combine the paddle training with cross training focused on strength training, stretching to stay limber, and cardio training.

In addition to paddleboard work, I have a daily morning routine that incorporates stretches, yoga poses, and push-ups. It does not require weights or any equipment, so I can do it even in a hotel room while traveling. It takes me less than 5 minutes to complete, and I try to do it every day before I have coffee and breakfast.

It's good to be consistent and stay fit year-round as it makes it easier to get back to peak performance for race season but it's also good to give the body a break occasionally. Listen to your body and don't overdo it.

Endurance training

When you're preparing for long-distance races, adding long, steady paddles at a maintainable pace of around 80 percent of your maximum effort conditions your stamina and endurance and prepares your body for the longer effort.

TIP

To avoid injury, don't do too much too fast. Start with a distance you can comfortably paddle at a good pace and then slowly increase the distance by no more than 10 percent per week.

Recovery

Letting your body rest and recover is as important as pushing your body to improve performance. A common mistake is to put off training and then overdo it before a race and not give your body enough time to recover. This tactic results in poor performance, so make sure to do the following:

>> Recover each day.

>> Eat well.

>> Get enough sleep (and take naps if you get tired during the day).

>> Avoid alcohol and drugs.

>> Schedule days with no training. If you have an intense training program to prepare for a big racing season, it's also a good idea to take a longer break for 1-2 months per year where you focus on recovery and don't push yourself hard in training.

"There's no such thing as over-training, only under-resting." – Deena Kastor

Be sure to balance that extended recovery with consistency, though. If you take *too* much time off from training, getting back into race shape takes longer. Training year-round keeps you in shape, which means preparing for a big race takes less effort.

Boosting performance

You can find many natural and scientifically proven ways to boost your performance, energy, and focus. Some things that have worked well for me over the years are Wim Hof breathing exercises, which I outline in Chapter 7; *contrast therapy* (sauna and cold plunge); intermittent fasting; and yoga.

When training for long races like the Molokai to Oahu race, I do weekly longer-distance training paddle sessions every weekend, starting with a distance of 6 to 8 miles and slowly increasing that by about 10 percent per week until I'm paddling close to the 32-mile race distance about a month before the race. (Ideally, I'm training in similar wind and water conditions to what I expect during the race as well.) Then I taper back on the training distance and focus more on speed and recovery as the big day approaches. The goal is to be well rested and at peak performance on race day.

Looking at Cross-Training

Although paddling is the best way to prepare for a paddle race, getting on the water consistently may not be possible for you. *Cross-training* in various disciplines is a good alternative for building strength, flexibility, balance, and endurance when you can't go paddling. It also keeps things interesting — variety is the spice of life! For example, in addition to SUP, I enjoy many other board sports, including *wing foiling* (a mashup of wind-surfing and kite surfing, using a handheld wing and hydrofoil under the board), surfing, and snowboarding. I also like going on long walks and challenging hikes, playing racquet sports, doing yoga, and strength training.

REMEMBER

Balanced nutrition and proper hydration play a critical role in training and racing performance. A diet rich in proteins, healthy fats, and carbohydrates fuels your workouts and helps with recovery.

Strength training

Building strength, particularly in your core, shoulders, back, and legs, is crucial for efficient paddling. Exercises such as planks, squats, and rowing help strengthen the important muscle groups for SUP. You can also add balance training to your strength training regimen by doing (for example) squats on a balance board. Incorporating resistance training with weights or resistance bands can enhance your power.

TIP

To avoid shoulder injuries, I routinely exercise my shoulder rotator cuff muscles by using external rotation exercises with resistance bands. External rotation exercises strengthen your rotator muscles and balance out the muscles in your shoulders to prevent injury from the repetitive internal rotation motion of SUP.

TECHNICAL STUFF

For a video demonstrating rotator cuff exercises, check out this YouTube video I made: youtu.be/QAOkU4sqQo0?si=Z8Tgr701PG EC1Q9N.

Cardiovascular workouts

Long-distance races demand cardio fitness. Running, hiking, cycling, and swimming are excellent ways to cross-train to build the endurance you need for racing. Aim for three or four cardio-vascular workouts per week, varying their intensity and duration so you can keep challenging your body.

Preparing Mentally

SUP racing is as much a mental challenge as it is a physical one, so preparing your mind is just as important as preparing your body.

REMEMBER

Mental toughness is crucial in racing. Be aware of your thoughts, and don't let negative self-talk take over when you start feeling fatigued. They can make keeping your balance harder and lead to poor technique. Here are some tips for staying in the right mindset:

>> **Keep your emotions in check.** Don't get too excited when things are going well, and don't get too frustrated when they aren't.

>> **Take deep breaths synchronized with your strokes.** Doing so helps with focus and can mean more consistent performance. I've found breathing exercises and meditation are good ways to be more aware of my thoughts and how they can influence me.

>> **Try visualization techniques.** Imagining yourself success-fully starting, navigating the racecourse, and crossing the finish line can boost your confidence and performance.

>> **Set realistic goals and celebrate small victories along your training journey to keep you motivated.** Entering in smaller races is also a great way to prepare for bigger, more important races as you get used to the added performance pressure of racing.

Being excited before the start of a race is fine, but many new racers can be overly nervous, with their hearts racing before the race even starts. Combat the nerves by being well prepared; getting to the start early; being fully set up and prepared well before the start; breathing deeply; hydrating well (see the later section "Nutrition and hydration"); and staying cool, calm, and collected.

Rounding up Race-Day Strategies

On race day, having a strategy is critical. Study the course and conditions. Think about how wind, waves, currents, temperature, and so on may play a role in the competition. Paddle the course before race day and make a mental note of the landmarks and distances to help plan your pacing. Be aware of the rules and practice the transitions like start, turns, and finish. If something isn't clear, ask at the pre-race meeting.

TIP

In flat water races, drafting behind one or more paddlers can save energy and allows you to keep a faster pace, but you need to practice drafting in training before attempting it in a race. If you're drafting, do your fair share of leading the pack, make sure you don't bump into the tail of the paddler in front, and make sure to follow the rules on drafting as they can vary by race.

Pacing

The start of a race is often a sprint, and you usually want to start fast to position yourself well in the field. Just keep in mind that you don't want to use up all your energy at the beginning of the race, so try to quickly find a comfortable, sustainable pace, breathing rhythm, and heart rate. Conserve your energy in the beginning of the race and gradually increase your effort as the event progresses. Running out of steam during a race and having others pass you toward the end is very demotivating.

I've found that training for SUP racing has motivated me to live a healthier lifestyle, which has improved my quality of life. Most people know what they need to do to be healthier: eating and hydrating properly; getting enough rest and sleep; having a good balance of work, personal, and family/friends time; getting enough exercise; staying limber; and limiting use of alcohol and drugs. Living a healthier lifestyle can result in better performance not only on the water but also in all aspects of your life, including improved energy, focus, stamina, and mental health off the water.

TIP

Particularly in downwind races, I find it best to focus on my own race and try not to let myself get too distracted or discouraged by competitors around me. (Sometimes chasing a paddler ahead of you can be helpful, though, and in flat water races drafting can be important.)

Nutrition and hydration

A comfortable hydration pack that allows you to sip while paddling is an essential piece of equipment for training paddles and races.

TIP

If I'm planning to be on the water for more than 30 to 45 minutes, I always bring a hydration pack along. Mixing electrolytes into the water helps replace minerals I lose by sweating and can prevent cramping. If you're paddling for more than two hours, you also need to bring easily digestible food (or liquid calories) to maintain peak performance over long distances.

Enjoying the Social Aspect of Training and Racing with Others

One of the most rewarding parts of SUP racing is the sense of community it fosters. Training and racing with friends can enhance your experience and provide an extra degree of motivation.

Training groups

Joining a SUP training group or club can provide you with a supportive network of fellow paddlers. Group training sessions offer a chance to learn from others, share tips and strategy, and push each other to improve. The camaraderie and the shared goals, struggles, and sense of accomplishment make the collective training experience more enjoyable and effective.

TIP

I've found a great way to get faster is by training with other paddlers who are at a level similar to yours. Having someone to chase after (or someone chasing you) is very motivating; it makes you push harder than you would if you were paddling by yourself. Paddling with others who are much faster or much slower than you doesn't provide the same incentive.

Racing events

Yes, SUP races are supremely competitive, but at their core, they're also deeply social gatherings. These events often include pre-race sign up, preparation, gear talk, socializing, and lots of post-race celebrations. The shared experience of competing creates a strong bond among participants and often leads to lasting friendships that extend beyond the shared sport. (I go more into enjoying the social aspects of paddling in Chapter 16.)

SUP racing is a dynamic and rewarding sport that challenges you to push your physical and mental limits in a supportive community of fellow enthusiasts. Whether you are competing for the thrill, the camaraderie, or the personal challenge, SUP racing has something to offer everyone. So, grab your paddle, hit the water, and experience the joys of SUP racing for yourself!

IN THIS CHAPTER

» Understanding etiquette in the surf

» Preparing for your first SUP surfing session

» Finding and getting into your surf stance

» Picking up the basics of paddling in the waves

» Catching and surfing waves

Chapter **13**

Conquering the Waves: SUP Surfing Technique

I love SUP surfing! It's a thrilling blend of stand up paddling and traditional surfing, and — here's a nice little SUP secret — the fact that you're already in a standing position makes it easier to paddle out, catch, and ride a wave without having to stand up while catching the wave. (And having the paddle for extra paddle power is an added bonus!)

Before you jump in, though, you need to make sure you've chosen suitable conditions and the right equipment, have understood surfing etiquette, and have practiced getting into surf stance, all of which I cover in this chapter. You also need to have gotten your forward and steering strokes down; if you haven't, flip to Chapter 11.

Always respect the ocean and your fellow surfers, and don't overestimate your abilities. See you in the surf!

Mastering Surfing Etiquette: How Not to Be That Paddler

Before you dive into the excitement of catching waves, I need to address the important topic of surfing etiquette. The following sections spell out some common-sense SUP surfing guidelines. For more on general SUP etiquette, head to Chapter 8.

Choosing the right spot

Ask other SUP surfers where you should go as a beginner or to take a lesson. When you're padding in open water, plenty of space is available for everyone, and most paddlers are very welcoming to newcomers — hey, the more, the merrier! Good surfing waves are a limited resource, however, and local surfers can often get very protective of their surf break.

If you see a surf spot that's crowded with skilled *shortboard* surfers (the traditional kind of surfing you're probably familiar with) and no stand up surfers, give the spot a hard pass and just keep looking. Not only are you not going to get a warm welcome, but your large board can also endanger others in the waves.

The ideal spot for learning to SUP surf is uncrowded and has small, rolling waves (slopey waves that break from the top of the wave rather than steep, fast breaking waves). The tide affects the waves, and some spots are busier in the morning or afternoon, so try to avoid the busy times and go when not a lot of other surfers are out.

Respecting the lineup

The *lineup* is the order in which surfers wait for waves. Don't paddle out past others and immediately try to catch a wave. Sit on your board away from the *peak* (the steepest part of the wave) and observe the lineup. The more experienced locals tend to get the best waves, but everyone waits their turn. As a beginner SUP surfer, you're lowest on the ladder, so be patient and wait your turn.

Avoiding dropping in

Dropping in means catching a wave that someone else is already riding, and it's a major no-no. The surfer who is closest to the peak has priority. Wait for a wave where you're closest to the peak, and don't commit to a wave until you make sure nobody closer to the peak is paddling for it.

Communicating

Smile and communicate with others. When you have a friendly attitude, you'll find that many surfers in the lineup are friendly and helpful. Let others catch some of the good waves and cheer them on. When a good wave comes to you, a simple "I'm taking this one" or "going left" can help prevent confusion and collisions.

Staying out of the way

When paddling out, avoid the path of other surfers; paddle around the break to stay clear. Be cognizant of the surfers around you. Your big board can do some damage if you fall off or have to bail while paddling through the waves.

REMEMBER

Be considerate, friendly, and patient. As a beginner, stay in less crowded areas where the waves are smaller and avoid crowded surf breaks. This tactic helps avoid conflicts and allows you to practice safely and without pressure.

Watch, Ask, and Learn: Before Going into the Surf

Preparation is key for a successful SUP surfing session. The following sections show you how to get ready before you jump in.

Observing the conditions

When you find a spot that's suitable for your skill level, spend some time watching the waves and currents. Notice the following:

>> Where the waves are breaking

>> Where surfers are positioning themselves to catch waves

>> Where others are entering and exiting the water

>> Where people paddle out

Waves generally come in sets of two to six bigger waves followed by smaller waves. Watch at least two sets come through so you have an idea of how big the sets are and how much time passes between the sets. The goal is to catch one of the set waves and then paddle back out during the lull between sets. Avoid catching a small wave before a set comes through as you can get "caught inside" which is when you get stuck the "impact zone" where the bigger set waves break on top of you. Also check out the Appendix, where more SUP surfing terms are explained.

Note any shallow areas and check whether the tide is rising or dropping. Avoid strong winds because the *wind chop* (small wind waves on the surface of the swell) makes balancing and surfing more challenging. Light offshore winds (wind blowing toward the waves) often result in beautiful, lined up waves with long *walls* (waves that stand up steep before breaking), but strong offshore winds can make catching a wave difficult as the wind pushes you backwards off the wave as you are trying to catch it. Onshore winds usually result in disorganized, choppy, crumbly waves that don't line up as well.

Waves break when they "touch" the bottom and, generally speaking, the height of the wave face when it starts to break is roughly the same as the water depth. That means that a small wave with a wave face of one to two feet breaks in water that's only about one to two feet deep. Because small waves are ideal for learning, you'll find yourself catching and surfing waves in shallow water. A sandy bottom is ideal (and safer) for beginners.

WARNING

Most surf spots in the tropics break over rocky reefs, which can be dangerous. Fall into the water flat (not feet first) so you don't go deep and be careful not to kick down when getting back on the board. Wearing booties is a good idea to protect your feet, but then, avoid stepping on the reef. To read more about falling safely, flip to Chapter 9.

TECHNICAL STUFF

If you do get a cut, make sure to clean it well. The live bacteria in the reef can get lodged in a cut and cause an infection that quickly ends your surfing adventure. Carefully clean cuts using soap to remove any particles and disinfect it with hydrogen peroxide.

Asking for advice

Don't hesitate to ask more experienced surfers or lifeguards about the local conditions, hazards, shallow areas, and currents and for other tips. Most are happy to share their knowledge.

Practicing on flat water

Before you hit the surf, make sure you're comfortable paddling, turning, and balancing on flat water. This approach gives you a good foundation and the confidence necessary for surfing.

As I mention in Chapter 11, practicing pivot turns in flat water is a good way to prepare yourself for surfing because it gets you used to switching your feet into surf stance (see the following section) and moving your weight back on the board, which is what you need to do when you're catching a cresting wave.

Going on *downwinders* (where you paddle with the wind and ride winds swells) is also a good way to prepare yourself for catching breaking waves. For more on downwinders, check out Chapter 16.

Surfing Regular versus Surfing Goofy Foot

Most people have a preferred position — regular or goofy — when riding on a board in *surf stance*.

>> **Regular foot:** Left foot forward, right foot back

>> **Goofy foot:** Right foot forward, left foot back

TIP

If you've never done any board sports and aren't sure what your natural stance is, stand up straight and have someone push you backward. The foot you instinctively move back to catch your fall is your back foot.

One of the most common mistakes SUP surfing beginners make is not switching into surf stance when catching a wave. As the board accelerates on the wave, they either *pearl* (where the nose of the board gets plowed underwater as the *tail* (back) gets lifted up by the wave) or fall backward as the board slides out underneath them. Getting into the surf stance allows you to shift your weight back to avoid pearling the nose while bracing yourself to keep from falling backward.

TIP

Switching to surf stance while catching a wave is one of the biggest challenges for beginners, so practice switching your feet from parallel stance (with the toes of both feet pointing forward, like on skis) to surf stance (with one foot forward and one back, like on a snowboard) on flat water. You can use the staggered stance, shown in Figure 13-1 (center) to transition from parallel stance to surf stance. You want to avoid putting all your weight on one rail (see Chapter 2) to keep the board from rocking. Try to rotate on the front heel and back ball and slowly shuffle your feet into surf stance, keeping your weight centered over the board.

FIGURE 13-1:
Parallel stance, staggered stance, and surf stance.

parallel stance

staggered stance

surf stance (regular foot)

If you're comfortable doing that, try to jump from parallel stance to surf stance (and back) in one quick movement. You can read more about getting into surf stance in the later section "Fancy Footwork: Switching Your Feet to Surf Stance." Practicing the pivot turn as explained in Chapter 11 is also a great way to practice your footwork.

REMEMBER

If you're paddling in flat water, which ankle you attach your paddleboard *leash* (safety strap) to doesn't really matter. But if you're surfing, always attach the leash to your natural back foot to avoid stepping on it.

Reading the Waves and Currents

Understanding wave behavior and currents is crucial for effective SUP surfing.

Types of waves

Observe how the waves break.

» *Soft* or *spilling* waves break more gently; when they peak, the top of the waves starts to crumble before they get very steep, and the whitewater rolls along. This type of wave usually breaks over a gently sloping bottom and is the most forgiving and best for learning.

» *Barreling* waves usually break on a shallow shelf where the bottom abruptly changes from deep water to shallow. This arrangement slows down the bottom of the wave while the top of the wave gets very steep. It *throws forward,* breaking from top to bottom with the *lip* (tip of the breaking wave) pitching forward and exploding into a wall of whitewater. Leave the barreling waves to the experts!

Rip currents

As the breaking waves push water in toward the shore, that water has to go somewhere. So it forms *rip currents* where the water flows back out to sea. Rip currents generally form between breaking waves, and you often find a deeper channel where the water runs out. As a SUP surfer, you can use these currents to paddle back out to the breaking waves. Observe the currents and see where others are paddling back out.

Swimmers often get caught in rip currents and wear themselves out trying to fight the current. If you ever find yourself in this situation, don't try to swim into the current. Instead, swim parallel to the shore to get out of the current and into the breaking waves that will push you back to shore.

Getting out There

Working your way past the *shore break* (waves breaking close to shore) and breaking waves to reach the lineup can be challenging. Here are some tips on how to do it:

>> **Launching:** Look at where others are launching in the water. Ideally, it's going to be a sandy spot with minimal waves. Walk out into knee-deep water, making sure the board's fins clear the bottom, and then hop onto the board.

>> **Dealing with shore break:** If you encounter breaking waves close to the shore, watch the sets and time your launch so you enter the water right after a set. Then quickly paddle out before the next set.

If shore break is an issue, paddling in a prone position with your arms (like on a surfboard) is often easiest. You can place your paddle blade under your chest with the shaft angled up and away from the board's nose. After you're through the waves, you can get on your knees or stand up and use the paddle.

>> **Paddling through breaking waves:** Surfers "duck dive" their boards under breaking waves to get out to the surf. Stand up paddleboards usually have too much volume to push under water, so the best way to get through breaking waves is by going over the whitewater.

To do so, paddle hard to gain some momentum, keeping the nose of the board pointed straight into the wave. Just before the whitewater hits you, quickly shift your weight back to pop the nose of the board up and over the whitewater. As the whitewater passes under you, quickly shift your weight forward again, brace your paddle for balance, and quickly start paddling to keep your forward momentum. *Note:* If the approaching whitewater is more than head-high, popping over it is very difficult.

If a wave is too big to go over and nobody's in the water behind you, you can jump off the board and dive deep under the wave with the board dragging on the leash behind you. Don't let go of your paddle. As the wave is dragging your board, you can brace your paddle as a rudder to bring you back to the surface.

Timing Is Everything: Catching a Wave

Catching a wave requires good positioning, paddle skills, and timing. Follow these steps:

Positioning

1. **Position yourself slightly outside the lineup, close to the peak.**

   As I note earlier in the chapter, the peak is the steepest part of the wave. I like to have the nose pointed toward the waves so I can turn left or right depending on where the wave is peaking.

Timing

2. **As the wave approaches, paddle with quick, powerful strokes to turn your board into the approaching wave.**

   The goal is to keep paddling on the same side and turn into the wave so your board points toward the beach just as you catch the cresting wave. You want to avoid turning too early; you don't want to switch sides with your paddle as you're catching the wave because you'll lose momentum and miss the wave.

Use your steering strokes and forward strokes (see Chapter 11) to control the speed of your turn into the approaching wave to avoid having to change sides with the paddle as you're catching the wave. Use quick, powerful forward strokes to gain momentum to match the speed of the wave.

Feel the lift

If you're positioned well, you'll feel the wave lifting and accelerating your board. Take a few more powerful strokes if necessary to catch the wave.

Fancy Footwork: Switching Your Feet to Surf Stance

Some people switch into surf stance before catching the wave, but I like to catch the wave in a slightly staggered stance (as in figure 13-1 above), then switch into surf stance as soon as I feel the board accelerating. The keys are to make the transition quickly and stay low.

Transitioning quickly

Quickly jump or shuffle into surf stance and move your weight toward the back of the board as you accelerate. This action keeps your nose from pearling and allows your board to start *planing* (sliding over the surface of the water), which also makes steering the board by leaning into a turn possible. If the wave slows down, you may have to shift your weight forward on the paddleboard to stay on the wave.

Staying low

Bend your knees and keep a low center of gravity for better balance. You can also lightly skim the paddle blade over the water surface to help you balance.

Riding Down the Line

Riding down the line means staying on the unbroken face of the wave rather than dropping straight down the wave and riding out the whitewater. Here's how you do it:

1. **Angle your board.**

   As you catch the wave, determine whether you can ride it to the left or the right and turn your board toward the *open face* — unbroken part of the wave. Staying higher on the wave helps you maintain speed on the face of the wave.

2. **Lean and steer.**

   Use your body weight to lean into the turn and steer your board. Lean forward to gain speed and back to turn harder or slow down. Skimming the paddle blade on the inside of the turn provides balance and allows you to turn tighter. (Essentially, you're using the paddle blade as a pivot point.)

Going for Bottom Turns and Cutbacks

When you're proficient enough to turn the board on takeoff and ride down the line (see the preceding section), you're ready to make your surfing more dynamic by making bottom turns and cutbacks.

» **Bottom turns:** A *bottom turn* is when you redirect your board from the base of the wave back towards the steeper part of the wave. As you accelerate down the wave to gain speed, lean into the bottom turn to redirect your board back up toward the face of the wave, leaning forward in the turn helps maintain speed, setting yourself up for a powerful cutback.

>> **Cutbacks:** A *cutback* is a tight turn on the top of the wave. As you come up the face of the wave, transition your weight to the opposite rail to turn back toward the breaking face of the wave. This move keeps you in the *power zone* — the steepest, most powerful part of the wave.

You can see bottom turns and cutbacks in the top and bottom of Figure 13-2, respectively. Note how the paddlers are bracing their paddles on the inside of the turns.

FIGURE 13-2: Skyla Rainer bottom turning and Tyler Judson cutting back.

Carrying out (Even More) Advanced Maneuvers

After you get the basics I cover earlier in the chapter down, you can try some of these more advanced moves:

>> **Top turn:** *Top turns* are like cutbacks (see the preceding section) but at the top of the wave. Lean into the turn, pivot

sharply off the tail of the board, and push with your legs to throw buckets of spray.

» **Reentry:** *Reentry (aka off the lip)* is a more advanced top turn where you turn on the breaking lip of the wave, ride out the turn on top of the breaking lip, complete the turn to reenter the open face of the wave, and set up for the next bottom turn (as covered above).

» **Floater:** A *floater* is similar to a reentry but involves riding over the top of the breaking wave before dropping back down into it.

» **360:** In this trick, you first move your weight forward and slide the board's fins out to turn the tail. Then you spin the board on the nose all the way around into a 360-degree turn.

ACCEPTING THE TRADE-OFFS OF SUP SURFBOARDS

As I got better at SUP surfing, I found that surfing on smaller, lower volume boards allowed me to surf better and turn harder. My boards got smaller and smaller over time, but at some point, paddling back out and catching waves on a tiny board became very challenging and frustrating. In the end it's all about having fun, so now I use a board I can comfortably paddle and catch waves on without sinking, even if it doesn't turn quite as well.

4

The SUP Lifestyle

Chapter **14**

The Unexpected Health Benefits of SUP

SUP is more than just a fun activity; it's a versatile and enjoyable way to stay fit.

Stand up paddleboarding has been a great way for me to get and stay in shape while having fun. I'm healthier and happier now than when I started SUPing back in 2008, and I love sharing the sport with others. Getting motivated to get on the water is easy for me (unlike going to a gym). For me, SUP has truly been a fountain of youth. If that's not convincing enough for you, I cover some of the many health benefits of SUP in this chapter.

REMEMBER

Embrace the challenge of the full-body workout, enjoy the scenic beauty, remember to have fun, and paddle yourself to a stronger, healthy, and happier you!

Paddling Your Way to a Better Bod

Paddling is not only a fun and exciting water activity but also a fantastic way to improve your overall fitness. The next few sections show how SUP can help you achieve a better physique.

Going for the full-body workout

From your toes to your fingertips, paddling in a standing position engages most of your muscle groups simultaneously. Balancing on your board activates your feet, legs, and glutes, while paddling engages your shoulders, arms, back, and core muscles. New paddlers often feel soreness in the bigger muscle groups as well as in small muscle groups, such as those in the feet, ankles, hands, and rotator cuffs; along the ribs; and more.

REMEMBER

Because SUP uses many muscles that you may not otherwise use much, even if you regularly exercise in a gym, you want to slowly acclimate your muscles to the new movements and not overdo it. Using good technique and the proper equipment is important; doing so not only is more efficient but also helps prevent injury, which can be caused by poor body mechanics and bad posture.

Improving cardiovascular health and endurance

Paddling and balancing increase your heart rate, providing an excellent cardiovascular workout. As you paddle, you're engaging in a form of cardiovascular exercise that strengthens your heart and lungs. Going on longer paddling excursions helps improve your heart health, endurance, and stamina over time.

To avoid injury, I find slowly increasing your distance and time on the water to be the best bet. A good guideline for endurance training is to add no more than 10 percent to your distance per week. To improve your endurance, aim to paddle for more than 45 minutes.

TIP

Using a heart rate monitor can help you track the intensity of your workout. Younger paddlers can sustain higher heart rates of up to 200 beats per minute (bpm). As age increases, the maximum heart rate decreases, but that doesn't mean older paddlers can't build up their endurance and paddle at a fast pace for long distances.

REMEMBER

The scenic environment, fresh ocean breezes, and thrill of getting away from your normal routine on land make paddling enjoyable. You may find yourself exercising longer and longer without even realizing it.

Opting for a low-impact exercise regimen

Unlike running or high-intensity interval training (HIIT), SUP is relatively gentle on your joints. The water is like a shock absorber, making it an ideal workout for people with joint issues who want a low-impact exercise option. Because paddling involves smooth, controlled movements, it's generally gentle on your joints while still promoting mobility in the knees, hips, spine, and shoulders. This aspect makes SUP a great therapeutic activity (with your physicians blessing, of course) for people recovering from injuries or those looking to maintain joint health and mobility as they get older.

Standing up from a kneeling position can be a bit challenging for people with knee problems, but after you're in a standing position, paddling strengthens your muscles while putting little strain on your joints. *Remember:* If you don't use it, you lose it.

Shedding Calories While Having Fun

One of the best things about SUP is that it doesn't feel like a workout, though it's a very effective way to burn calories.

Depending on your intensity level, paddling at a normal pace can burn around 300 to 500 calories per hour. More vigorous paddle training, tackling rough water, SUP surfing in challenging conditions, or chasing *bumps* (wind waves) on a downwind paddle can significantly increase the number of calories burned. (You can read more about SUP surfing in Chapter 13.)

When you're going on longer paddles of over an hour, refueling by replacing some of the calories burned can be helpful; doing so allows you to perform at a higher level for longer. I touch on food and hydration in Chapter 7, but preferences vary by the individual paddler. When I go on long training paddles or compete in races, I like to bring easily digestible snacks, such as energy bars, gels, or chews.

REMEMBER

Paddling can motivate you to live a healthier lifestyle; you may even find yourself craving healthy, nutritious food after paddling.

GET THE STRESS OUT

SUP has been a great way for me to stay in shape mentally as well. Stepping into the liquid element, I unplug from my normal life and plug into nature. If I take a phone for safety reasons, I mute it to eliminate distractions. The water has a calming effect, immediately reducing my stress and promoting mental well-being and positive thoughts.

Lower stress levels contribute to overall health and can also help with weight management. Balancing on your board requires attention and forces you to be in the moment. Focusing on your stroke technique and breathing can have a meditative effect, calming your mind. Many paddlers enjoy listening to music or podcasts (through waterproof headphones) while paddling. I like to just listen to the sounds around me and be present in the moment.

Better than a Six Pack: Contributing to Core Strength

A strong core is essential for overall fitness, and SUP is one of the most effective ways to build and maintain core strength. Unlike traditional exercises that isolate specific muscles, SUP provides a dynamic workout that challenges your balance and stability and engages multiple muscle groups simultaneously. The movement patterns work to strengthen your core while improving other key areas of fitness.

Bringing in balance and stability

The balance and stability required for good paddling technique strengthen and tone your abdominal, oblique, and lower back muscles in a variety of ways:

>> Maintaining balance on the board and transferring power from the paddle to the board requires continuous engagement of your core muscles.

>> As I discuss in Chapter 11, good stroke technique entails pushing down on the paddle, using your abdominal muscles, and working with gravity as you apply pressure to the paddle blade.

>> Every paddle stroke requires your body to make fine adjustments to stay stable on the water, continuously engaging those same core muscles as balance does.

SUP activates these muscles in a way that's difficult to replicate using traditional exercises. As you fine-tune your stroke technique, the continuous action of your core can lead you toward that six-pack look while also improving your balance and posture.

Building functional strength

Improved core strength isn't just about aesthetics. Traditional core exercises like crunches, sit-ups, and planks isolate specific muscle groups. SUP builds *functional strength*; it trains your core muscles in a way that mimics real-life movements, allowing your body to become more efficient at handling everyday tasks from lifting groceries to climbing stairs to bending to pick up a heavy item. Functional core strength also protects against injury by stabilizing your body during unpredictable, awkward, or sudden movements.

Enhancing performance in other areas

A strong core translates into better performance in other sports and physical activities. Whether you're running, riding a bike, or lifting weights, having a strong, stable core provides a good foundation for improved efficiency and power.

REMEMBER

You may soon notice improvements in other sports when you *cross-train* in other disciplines. For example, runners may notice better coordination, posture, and endurance, while weightlifters can experience greater stability during deadlifts. Even heavy-duty tasks, such as moving furniture or loading construction materials, feel easier as your strong core from paddling helps you stabilize and control these movements more effectively.

Improving Muscle Control and Coordination

SUP does more than just build muscle strength; it also helps improve muscle coordination and control. Paddling engages multiple muscle groups in a smooth, continuous motion, forcing your brain to fine-tune how these muscles work together.

Focusing on balance training

One of the most significant benefits of paddling in a standing position is its role in improving balance. SUP requires constant fine adjustments that engage the stabilizer muscles in your legs, core, and upper body, which all have to work together to generate smooth, powerful, balanced movements.

TIP

As your balance improves, you can challenge yourself further in a few ways:

>> Using narrower boards

>> Going out in more challenging conditions

>> Training on a wobbly board

These progressions not only improve your balance on the board but also enhance your overall coordination and balance, which are important for everyday activities and other sports, especially other board sports.

REMEMBER

You weren't born with poor balance; balance can be trained, just like strength can. If you gradually and consistently increase the balance challenge over time, your body will adapt and become better at balancing.

Targeting neuromuscular coordination

Unlike lifting weights, which targets specific muscles, the fine motor control required for SUP promotes better *neuromuscular* (brain-to-muscle) coordination. Paddling on a moving surface while maintaining balance takes neuromuscular coordination to the next level. SUP strengthens the connections between your brain and your muscles, enabling you to execute movements with more precision.

The refined muscle coordination that comes from paddling translates into smoother, more efficient movement patterns in other sports and physical activities. Plus, improving neuromuscular coordination can help prevent injuries by allowing your muscles to react quickly and appropriately to sudden changes in your environment.

Reflecting on reflexes

The unpredictable nature of water demands that your body constantly adjust to changes in surface conditions. The quick adjustments needed to navigate sudden water movements train your reflexes, resulting in faster reaction times. Whether you're quickly recovering from an unexpected chop hitting your board by bracing with your paddle or by adjusting your weight placement, SUP helps you develop sharp reflexes that can be beneficial in many everyday situations and other athletic activities.

Adding Up the Additional Health Benefits of SUP

I discuss many benefits of stand up paddleboarding in the other sections of this chapter, but they don't cover all of it. Here are a few extra health benefits you should consider as you venture into the world of SUP:

» **Mental clarity, better focus, and better sleep:** For many people, SUP isn't just a workout; it's a mental retreat. I've found that getting out on the water allows me to disconnect from the stresses of daily life, thus clearing my mind and reducing anxiety and stress. The calming effect of being in nature combined with the rhythmic pattern of the strokes helps enhance focus and mental clarity.

Many people also report better sleep after a day of stand up paddleboarding, thanks to the calming effect of both physical exercise and time spent outdoors.

» **Flexibility:** The dynamic movements required when paddling in a standing position promote flexibility in key areas. As you reach forward with each stroke, your muscles stretch and lengthen between contractions, encouraging flexibility over time (especially in your hips, lower back, and shoulders). Regular SUP practice can enhance your range of motion, making you more limber and reducing inflammation and stiffness in your joints.

» **Vitamin D:** Yes, vitamin D. Spending time outdoors on the water exposes you to sunlight, which helps your body produce vitamin D. This essential vitamin plays a crucial role in maintaining bone health, regulating your immune system, and boosting your mood. Just remember not to overdo sun exposure when the UV index is high because of the obvious risks involved when you soak up too many of the sun's rays. For tips on protecting yourself from too much sun, check out Chapter 6.

Chapter **15**

Finding Your Paddle Tribe: Enjoying the Sport Socially

P addling by yourself can be a soulful experience, but sharing the fun with others can make the practice even more memorable and enjoyable. The shared passion for the sport creates a unique bond among paddlers. In this chapter, I explore how you can turn your SUP experience into a more social and communal activity, finding your "paddle people" along the way.

REMEMBER

By getting involved in the social side of SUP, you discover that paddling is much more than a solitary activity; it's an incredible way to connect with others, build lasting friendships, and create unforgettable memories on the water. Regardless of which discipline you choose, the SUP community is waiting for you to join in the fun.

Adding More Bodies to The Mix

"Being social" can mean different things to different people. For the more introverted, it means having some special one-on-one time with a certain friend of the two-legged or four-legged variety. For others, it means the more, the merrier. I try to cover all possibilities in the following sections.

Paddling with a single passenger

Paddleboarding solo is a blast, but many SUP enthusiasts enjoy sharing the experience with a child or friend. When you add a passenger, the shared experience is extra special.

When paddling with a passenger, balance is key. Here are a few tips:

>> **Larger, wider boards designed for stability with a long deck pad are the best choice.** Keep in mind that the board needs to float the combined weight of both you and the passenger, so it needs extra volume. Expect the board to be extra tippy with the added weight and movements from a passenger, especially if the passenger stands up or moves around unexpectedly.

>> **Ask the passenger to avoid quick movements.** When the paddler or the passenger make unexpected movements, it can throw off both people's balance. This situation can lead to overcorrecting, which usually ends with both falling in (so be ready to get wet!). Ideally, both the paddler and the passenger make small balance adjustments only and keep movements to a minimum.

>> **Have the passenger sit slightly forward of the center of the board.** As the paddler, you can position yourself behind the passenger, making sure to place your weight so the board is *trimmed* well — level with the water surface, in other words.

>> If standing up is too challenging, stay seated or on your knees to keep the center of balance lower.

REMEMBER

Both people can stand up and paddle, but that takes even better coordination. Start with the passenger sitting down on the front of the board with minimal movement while the person in the back paddles.

WARNING

When paddling with a passenger, be careful when changing sides with the paddle so you don't bang it into the passenger.

SUPing together on big boards

Paddling with a group of people on one giant board is a blast! Also known as SUPsquatch or MegaSUP boards, these super-sized inflatable boards are built to hold four to ten paddlers. They require synchronized strokes and communication to keep them going in the right direction, so teamwork is a must. SUPs-quatch paddling is a great way to connect with the other paddlers on the board through the shared experience.

The annual Buffalo Big Board Surfing Classic has a SUPsquatch division where teams compete in big waves at Makaha Beach on Oahu's West Side, and it's one of the most popular events. (When used to ride waves, a *steersman* with fins rides in the back and acts as a rudder to steer the board like a giant body board.) Some SUP races also have divisions for teams paddling these extra-large boards. For more on fueling your competitive urges, check out the following section.

Getting into the Competitive Spirit

Nothing builds social bonds quicker than being on a team together, working toward a common goal. (That common goal being, of course, *beating the other teams!*) The next few sections look at ways stand up paddleboarding can build team spirit.

SUP polo

If you're looking for a new way to hone your SUP skills while having fun and good-natured competition with friends, SUP polo is a great way to connect with other paddlers, build friendships, and get a great workout. Like water polo, *SUP polo* is a fast-paced, high-energy game where two teams try to hit a ball into the opposing team's goal — in this case, by using the paddle. I've been playing games with a group that meets weekly, and it's a blast!

SUP polo requires quick reflexes, agility, and solid balance. You also need some particular skills:

>> Paddling skills, such as

- Quick acceleration and sprinting

- Directional control

- Pivoting the board

- Maintaining balance under pressure

>> Skills specific to SUP polo, such as

- Handling the ball by using your paddle

- Passing

- Teamwork

- Situational awareness

- Offensive and defensive strategies

As a bonus, the quick sprints required result in a surprisingly good workout.

An official SUP polo setup includes inflatable field boundaries and goals with nets. Official rules allow the ball to be played with a paddle from a standing position only and don't allow body contact with the ball.

REMEMBER

SUP polo boards are usually fairly short for good maneuverability and relatively wide for stability. Soft top boards (hard boards with a soft foam outer layer) are good because they're less likely to get damaged in collisions; the preferred board of the group

I play with is a soft top SUP that's 9 feet 6 inches long and 34 inches wide. Inflatable boards are also a good option (see Chapter 3).

Using protective gear is a good idea, and some players wear water shoes and helmets to protect from impacts with other players, boards, and paddles, as well as knee pads to protect from chafing if they're paddling in a kneeling position.

Paddles made specifically for SUP polo have a hole in the blade. These special SUP polo paddles work much like a lacrosse stick and make picking up, passing, and even catching the ball with the paddle easier. The group I play with just plays with regular SUP paddles, which also works fine. Picking up the ball from the water surface with a regular SUP blade takes some skill, though, so practice this skill before playing a game.

The trick to lifting the ball off the water surface is to get the blade directly under the ball, level to the water surface, with no water between the ball and the blade before lifting it up. If you have any water between the blade and the ball, the ball tends to get washed off the blade surface. After you've lifted the ball off the water surface, you can bounce and hit it with the paddle blade to pass it to an open player or hit it toward the goal.

TIP

You can change up SUP polo to meet your needs. For example, our group simply uses two inflatable swim rings as goals, anchored using small weights. If the ball touches the ring, it's one point; if the ball goes inside the ring, it counts as two points. We also play with modified rules that allow playing the ball from a kneeling position, hitting the ball (but not holding or lifting it) with our hands or feet, and board-to-board contact (but not paddle-to-board contact).

SUP races

Competing in SUP races isn't just about speed and endurance; it's an opportunity to connect with other paddlers. Whether you're at a local fun race or an international event, you encounter a sense of community that brings everyone together. Everyone enjoys talking about the conditions, the course, gear used, technique, and race strategy.

Before a race, you can find paddlers swapping tips, sharing stories, talking about the latest and greatest equipment, and encouraging one another, regardless of skill level. After the finish line, the community usually gathers for an awards ceremony to celebrate achievements, eat and drink, reflect on performances, talk about their take-aways, and simply enjoy the shared experience. The social aspect extends beyond the competition itself; SUP racing is a small, close-knit community, and you'll recognize many of the same faces at various local races.

One of the most memorable SUP races I've participated in was the SUP 11-City Tour in the Netherlands. It's a five-day day race along canals through the picturesque Dutch countryside. Participants live on a boat that follows the paddlers along the roughly 136-mile-long course. I didn't know any other participants when I signed up for this race. The sense of community from living, eating, talking, and sleeping together on a boat and the shared experience of struggling through the long days of paddling resulted in many new friendships with paddlers from all over the world.

RELAY RACING

Relay races are an excellent way to foster team building for all levels of paddlers. At Blue Planet Surf, we often host bigger groups of paddlers, and a fun way to end the group lesson is to hold a relay race. We split the group into two or more teams, and each team member must paddle from the beach out to a buoy and back before passing the board to the next team member until the whole team completes one leg of the relay. Teamwork is essential, and the excitement builds as the teams cheer each other on as each leg is completed. It's a memorable group activity for corporate team-building exercises, family reunions, and birthday parties. It's also a great way for first-time paddlers to apply the new skills they've just learned.

Being Together for the Sake of Being Together

Whether you're training for a race or just paddling for fun, going out with a group is another excellent way to socialize while enjoying the water. Always going for the win can be incredibly draining. Competitiveness has its place, but sometimes the bonds you create when coming together with others can be equally beneficial. (Just think of all the team-building exercises you may have experienced in school — don't forget the school of life — or at work.)

Training groups

When you're training for races, paddling with others is an effective way to see how your technique and equipment stack up as you paddle close to others in the same conditions.

TIP

I find going out with a group of other motivated paddlers makes training regularly, getting motivated, maintaining a fast pace, and paddling for longer distances much easier. Scheduling a regular meeting time and place makes maintaining and improving your paddling skills and fitness a breeze.

Paddling as a group can also prepare you for actual races because you can incorporate a mock race as part of the training group. Create a set course that includes a start, transitions, drafting, and a finish line. You can compare your performance against other paddlers in your group and time yourself to see whether you're making improvements over time.

REMEMBER

Even when you're paddling the same course, conditions often change thanks to wind and currents, so your finish time alone isn't always a good indicator of your performance. Paddling with someone who's close to you in speed allows you to see directly whether you're improving and also pushes everyone else in the group to keep upping their game.

Trolling groups

If competitive paddling isn't your cup of tea, no worries! Leisurely group paddles are another excellent way to socialize and connect with other paddle enthusiasts. Many paddlers form groups that meet regularly for *trolling* sessions — long, relaxed paddles on lakes, rivers, or the ocean. These outings aren't about speed or distance; they're about soaking in the scenery, enjoying the company of other paddlers, and maybe stopping for a coffee or snack along the way.

These group trolling paddles are especially common in popular SUP destinations. The slower pace is ideal to have conversations, swap tips, and enjoy the serenity of being outdoors together. They're also a good opportunity to introduce beginners to the sport because they present less pressure to keep up, paddling as a group is safer than paddling alone, and everyone is there simply to have fun.

TIP

Joining or creating a leisure paddle group that meets regularly can deepen your connection to the SUP community and introduce you to new friends who share your passion for the sport. It's also a fantastic way to safely explore new waterways and routes that you may not have discovered on your own. You can find out about local paddle groups though SUP schools and retailers, Facebook groups, meetup groups, or start your own group will fellow paddlers.

Connecting with Others

SUP is more than just a sport; it's a community. Countless resources are available for paddlers to connect with one another, whether you're looking to improve your skills, find a paddling partner, or join a local paddle group or club. Here are just some of the options:

>> Most popular paddle destinations have SUP-specific events, such as group paddles, races, classes, meetups, and charity events. These gatherings attract like-minded people and are a great way to connect with fellow paddlers and develop friendships on and off the water.

>> Online forums and social media groups offer a platform for paddlers to exchange tips, share experiences, and find out about events in their areas. You can find resources to connect with others in Chapter 23.

>> Messaging groups or text threads are another popular way to share updates on conditions, events, meetups, photos, and video within smaller groups of paddlers.

REMEMBER

Whether you're just starting out or are already an experienced paddler, you'll find that the SUP community is supportive and welcoming. From local paddling meetups to events around the world, you have so many opportunities to connect with others who share your love for the sport.

Chapter **16**

SUP Racing: Going for the (Olympic) Gold

A s a result of the growing popularity of SUP, discussions about whether the sport deserves a place in the Olympic arena have been ongoing. In this chapter, I look at the developments in SUP's Olympic status (as of this writing) and what potential SUP events you may see in future Games.

The Long Road to Olympic Glory

Two organizations — the International Canoe Federation (ICF) and the International Surfing Association (ISA) — have been battling over who should govern SUP at the highest level. In 2020, the independent Court of Arbitration for Sport (CAS) ruled that the ISA is responsible for governing and administering SUP at the Olympic level, so the surfers won out over the canoers.

The International Olympic Committee (IOC) sealed the deal by officially recognizing the ISA as the sport's governing body. The ICF hasn't been shut out completely, however; both organizations continue to put on international events, such as the Pan American Games and the World Beach Games, demonstrating that the IOC was right to recognize the appeal of SUP.

Although SUP wasn't included in the Paris 2024 games, the ISA continues to promote SUP and hopes to make it an Olympic sport in the 2028 Los Angeles Olympic Games and the 2032 Brisbane Olympic Games.

Including SUP in the Olympics would bring numerous benefits to the sport and its community, including greater visibility and popularity on a global scale, more funding from national sports associations, and increased youth participation, not to mention sponsorship opportunities, professionalization of the sport, and global standardization of formats, equipment, and rules.

REMEMBER

SUP has become very popular in countries with strong watersports cultures, such as the United States, Australia, and parts of Europe, but Olympic inclusion could lead to rapid growth in countries where it's less well known, inspiring the next generation to SUP not just as a recreational hobby but as a serious athletic pursuit.

Surfing into the Olympics

Because SUP is rooted in surfing, the ISF will certainly push to include SUP surfing as an Olympic discipline, especially now that surfing is an Olympic sport. The SUP surfing format would most likely be similar to the surfing format, which made its debut at the 2020 Tokyo Olympics (held in 2021 due to COVID-19 restrictions).

TECHNICAL STUFF

The surfing competition at the Paris 2024 Olympics wasn't held in France but rather on the other side of the world, in the big, barreling waves at Teahupo'o in Tahiti. (See Figure 16-1.) As you'd expect given the tropical venue, it was quite exciting to watch.

FIGURE 16-1:
The surfing contest at the Paris 2024 Olympics.

Typical SUP surfing contests are judged on the following:

>> Wave selection

>> Maneuvers

>> Power

>> Speed

>> Flow

>> Innovation

>> Progress

>> Control

>> Style

A panel of judges scores each wave on a scale of one to ten, with ten being a perfect score. Usually only a rider's two best waves are counted toward the final score, and there is a system that gives the surfer with priority the right to catch the next wave to ensure fair wave distribution. Paddlers need to select the best waves to catch as the quality of the waves ridden can have a big impact on the score. The SUP surfers with the highest combined score advance to the next round, while the riders with the lower scores are eliminated.

The Thrill of Victory: SUP Racing for King and Country

In addition to SUP surfing (see the preceding section), SUP racing will likely be included when SUP joins the Olympics. Because racing doesn't depend on waves, you can practice it anywhere in the world. That makes it a good candidate to become a truly global sport, especially if it's included in the Olympics. In the following sections, I walk you through some of the most popular SUP race formats currently practiced and some major existing events in those disciplines.

Flatwater racing

Flatwater racing in relatively calm and smooth water is the most accessible and beginner-friendly race format. Courses can range from short sprints (as short as 100 meters) to long-distance races that take several hours to complete. The start is usually either a beach start or a line in the water marked by buoys/a boat. Although you may have some buoys to navigate within the course, most of the race consists of paddling in a straight line between points.

REMEMBER

Don't be fooled by how leisurely that may sound, though. At the competitive level, flatwater races are highly strategic, with tactics such as *drafting* — riding in the wake of another paddler to reduce drag — and navigating quick turns around buoys playing a significant role in the race outcomes. You also need solid endurance and paddle technique.

Boards used in flatwater racing, such as the one shown in Figure 16-2, are generally sleek and sport narrow displacement hull shapes (which I cover in Chapter 2). Athletes need to have good balance to ride these boards; they also need to maintain an optimal stroke rate and efficient stroke technique to conserve energy and stay in a straight line because veering off the course results in lost time.

LIKE DUCKS IN A ROW: DRAFTING TO SAVE ENERGY

The first time I drafted behind another paddler, I was surprised by how much less energy it took to maintain a faster pace in somebody else's wake. Drafting on a SUP is similar to bicycle racers who draft by taking advantage of the wind shadow created by the lead cyclist. When you closely follow behind a lead paddler, the water is smoothed out and pulled forward by the lead board, resulting in less drag and less energy needed to maintain the speed. This drafting effect seems to be even more pronounced in the third or fourth position. Drafting with several boards in a row effectively lengthens the waterline and a longer waterline reduces drag. (See Chapter 3 for more on this topic.)

While it takes less energy to maintain a fast pace, drafting requires intense focus. The tricky part is to maintain a close distance to the board in front of you without bumping into the tail and without going off course. I focus on the tail in front of me and usually switch my paddle one or two strokes after the lead paddler does, while constantly adjusting the power of my stokes to maintain the right speed and using steering strokes (if needed) to stay directly behind the paddler in front of me. I would estimate that drafting uses 10 to 20 percent less energy, which is significant. If you are drafting in a race, be sure to follow race rules; some races don't allow drafting or only allow drafting behind other paddlers with the same board length or division.

Technical racing

Technical races are usually held in more dynamic coastal or beach settings, where competitors navigate a course marked by buoys that usually leads through the *surf zone* — the area where the waves are actually breaking. These races may also include a run on the beach between laps and tight turns around buoys and other obstacles.

FIGURE 16-2: Narrow boards are faster but also difficult to balance on.

SUP'S DISTANT OLYMPIC COUSIN

As I write this, the closest Olympic sport to SUP racing is Canoe Single, where athletes kneel in the boat and use a single-bladed paddle on one side at a time as in the figure shown here. The skills, technique, and athleticism in this sport are similar to SUP racing, and it's no surprise that former Olympic canoeists Larry Cain and Jim Terrell have become elite-level SUP racers.

Technical races add a layer of complexity for competitors, which means paddlers have to be highly versatile to succeed. Skills needed for technical races include the following:

>> Reading the water conditions and making tactical and timing decisions when catching a swell or paddling out through breaking waves

>> Maintaining balance and agility in tight turns

>> Avoiding collisions

>> Being able to accelerate quickly after transitions

The exciting and spectator-friendly technical race format was pioneered by the Battle of the Paddle race in Dana Point, California in 2008 and has become a common race format at many events.

Downwind racing

Downwind racing is my favorite SUP race format because it combines both racing and surfing skills, and experience and skill often trump endurance and stamina. Downwind races are held in windy conditions where the wind blowing over the water surface creates *bumps* — rolling swells that racers can ride. In Hawaii, these races are held in the open ocean, but they can also occur in lakes and in rivers, such as the Columbia River Gorge, as long as the wind blows consistently and pushes paddlers along the course.

Downwind races use a combination of paddle and wave-riding skills. The key to going fast in downwind races is reading the water surface and harnessing the bumps to propel the board forward. To time your strokes correctly, you have to paddle hard to accelerate and catch a good bump when the opportunity presents itself and then glide on the bump and rest. On the open ocean, swells usually come from different angles and vary in height and steepness. The goal in downwind racing is to conserve energy by riding the waves efficiently and resting while gliding on the swell, saving energy for the sprint effort needed to catch the next fast-moving bump. Therefore, being able to read the water surface and knowing when to paddle hard and when to rest is often more important than the paddling strength and endurance that matter most in the flatwater and technical races I cover in earlier sections.

Unlike SUP surfing, where you look back to see the approaching swell, you need to keep your gaze forward when catching bumps. *Wind swell* — the small waves created by wind blowing over the surface of the water — have a short period, meaning the distance between two wave peaks is small. Unlike wind swell that is created by local winds, breaking waves in the surf zone are often created by storms far away and travel a long distance before breaking over a shallow bottom. These waves (also known as *ground swell*) have a longer period, so they are not steep in deep water and only get steep when the wave slows down over a shallow bottom. Short period wind swells on the other hand can get quite steep even in deep water.

When riding wind swells on a downwinder, I try to chase the back side of a good bump in front of me until it pulls me along, then I stop paddling and glide on the bump. The skill of reading the water means watching the water surface and waiting for the right moment to paddle hard to catch a steep bump, using it to glide as far and fast as possible, and then maintaining the speed to connect into the next glide to maintain a high average speed.

The most popular downwind race in Hawaii is the Da Hui Paddle Race (shown in Figure 16-3), held every July 4 on Oahu's North Shore. The short course starts at Sunset Beach while the long course starts at the Turtle Bay resort; the finish for both courses is Waimea Bay. In the summer, the water is calm and clear, and the trade wind breezes push paddlers along, making the short course a great race for first-time SUP racers. (During the winter surf season, this famous coastline has some of the biggest, heaviest waves in the world.)

The Molokai to Oahu (M2O) race, is regarded as one of the most challenging downwind races and is known as the Paddleboard World Championships. It started as a prone paddleboard race in 1997 but has included a SUP division since 2006.

FIGURE 16-3:
The start of
the Da Hui
Paddle Race
on July 4,
2024.

I've been competing in this 32-mile race across the Ka'iwi channel since 2009, and the unique physical and mental challenges it poses has long served as great motivation for my training. (My fastest time was 5 hours and 27 minutes, while my slowest time was 6 hours and 45 minutes, in case you were wondering.) Paddling and balancing on this rough stretch of ocean for that long takes not only endurance but also mental focus, stamina, and strategy.

GAINING GROUND IN THE M2O

With the advent of downwind SUP foiling (see Chapter 24), many riders at the Molokai to Oahu (M2O) race have switched to this faster and even more challenging discipline. This departure has led to fewer entries in the SUP division, although a hardcore group of downwind SUP paddlers keeps coming back for the challenge year after year, including me. With fewer top-level athletes entering the race, placing in the standings has become easier, and in 2024 (my 13th time competing in this race), I unexpectedly won the stock SUP division — my best result ever.

The decrease in racers hasn't made the M2O a cakewalk, though. In addition to the physical and mental challenge, competing in this inter-island race is a logistical challenge. Each competitor must hire their own escort boat and captain; arrange board transportation, airfare, and accommodations; and plan for hydration and nutrition requirements. Having to overcome all these obstacles and suffering through the race is part of what makes it such a memorable and rewarding experience.

Adventure/endurance racing

Adventure races not only test your physical abilities but also require strategic planning, navigation, and survival skills. You have to rely on experience, intuition, and grit to overcome fatigue and navigate remote, unfamiliar waters in unpredictable weather conditions. Here are just some of the things you have to juggle:

>> **Nutrition/hydration:** Nutrition and hydration strategies play an important role. *Tip:* Eat before you feel hungry and drink before you feel thirsty. In the case of a fast-moving river like the Yukon, paddlers often choose to eat and rest sitting on the board while moving downstream with the current rather than sitting still on land.

>> **Sleep strategy:** Races on the Yukon are so far north that the sun never sets, so you may be tempted to keep paddling through the night. But as the sleep deficit grows, some participants may experience confusion, disorientation, brain fog, and even pangs of paranoia and hallucinations (that's sleep deprivation for you).

>> **Supply logistics:** Many of these races require participants to carry essential supplies, including safety gear, drinking water, and food supplies. The logistics of getting to the start with all the necessary gear and support is part of the challenge.

Long distance adventure racing isn't for the faint of heart; it attracts athletes who are looking not only for competition but also for an adventure where they can explore some of the world's most stunning and remote natural locations.

Although the M2O race I cover in the preceding section qualifies as an endurance race that pushes athletes to their absolute limits, other ultra-endurance SUP races span much longer distances and often take place over several days. Popular adventure/ultra-endurance races include these:

>> **The Yukon 1000, known as The World's Longest Paddle Race:** This race covers roughly 1,000 miles (1,600 kilometers) from Canada to Alaska, and its extreme nature gives it a reputation as one of the toughest endurance races.

Two-person teams paddle unassisted with all their gear from Whitehorse, Yukon, Canada, to the Dalton Highway Bridge in Alaska (which is in the Arctic Circle). Paddlers take six to nine days to complete this course.

>> **The Yukon River Quest, known as The Race to the Midnight Sun:** This competition covers 444 miles (714 kilometers) through the Canadian wilderness from Whitehorse to Dawson City (also in the Yukon territory) along the fast-moving Yukon River.

>> **The SUP 11-City Tour:** This race in the Netherlands covers 136 miles (220 kilometers) over five days. In addition to the five-day tour, this competition also has a nonstop division where paddlers complete the whole course without sleep in over 24 hours.

>> **The Last Paddler Standing:** This SUP-only endurance race takes place in Sarasota, Florida. Racers paddle a 3.33-mile loop (5.4 kilometers), starting and finishing within a one-hour period. Additional loops start every hour on the hour. At the 48-hour mark, the loop distance increases to 4.9 miles. The race goes on until only one finisher is left. In 2023, the winner completed 50 loops after paddling 170 miles over 50 hours without sleep.

REMEMBER

Preparing and training for one of these races can take years. If adventure/ultra-endurance racing sounds like your cup of tea, set a goal, make a long-term plan, take baby steps toward your goal, and start training!

Chapter 17

Taking Care of Your Board: Maintenance and Repair

I f you use your board regularly, you'll inevitably expose it to heat, UV rays, bumps, scratches, and worse. In this chapter, I go over how to properly take care of your board, including information about regular maintenance, DIY repairs, professional repairs, and advanced board construction.

Note: I introduce the construction basics in Chapter 3, but my goal in this chapter is to cover some additional aspects of construction that help you understand why maintaining your board is important. If it sparks an interest that leads to you researching more or even sets you on the path to start shaping and building your own boards, great.

Pride of Ownership: Zen and the Art of Board Maintenance

Inflatable boards (iSUPs) and hard boards have very different construction and maintenance, so I treat them separately in this chapter. I start with inflatable boards because they're the more commonly used option. If you have a hard board, you can head straight to the section "Peeking at What's under the Glass: The Anatomy of a Hard Board," where the hard board discussions begin.

Eyeing iSUP Board Construction, Maintenance, and Repair

As I explain in Chapter 3, inflatable boards are made using drop-stitch technology, which keeps the deck and bottom of the board flat under pressure. After the iSUP is filled up with air at the right pressure (usually between 15 and 25 pounds per square inch, or psi), the board goes from being a floppy taco to something rigid enough to paddle on with minimal flex.

REMEMBER

Manufacturers use many tricks and gimmicks to add rigidity, but generally speaking, the thicker the drop-stitch material is (thickness of the board) and the higher the pressure it can be pumped up to, the more rigid the board is.

REMEMBER

Yes, you can just get a cheap "disposable" inflatable board that you don't have to maintain, but please also consider the environmental impact of the petrochemical products that make up these boards landing in a landfill. In the long run, buying a higher quality board and taking good care of it is a better value.

The inflation valve

Most iSUPs have a Halkey-Roberts valve (shown in Figure 17-1) that's designed to keep the pressure inside where it belongs when you need it most. You can let the air out by pushing in and twisting the valve stem clockwise to lock it in the open position. The valve does a pretty good job of holding the air pressure in on its own, but it does have a protective cap to cover the valve while in use.

Because the drop-stitch threads aren't attached where the valve is, the surface directly underneath the valve forms a bit of a bubble on the bottom of the board. That's not a defect; it's completely normal. All iSUPs have a small bubble directly beneath the valve.

TIP

Make sure to close the valve before inflating the board by twisting the spring-loaded valve stem counterclockwise so it pops up. (The valve is closed in that position and will keep the pressure inside the board.) If you leave the valve in the open position, it lets out the pressure as soon as you remove the pump, and you have to start pumping all over again. This goof is a terribly frustrating experience, but it's one that's happened to the best of paddlers.

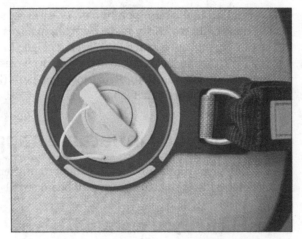

FIGURE 17-1:
A Halkey-Roberts valve with valve cover attached.

lilkin/Adobe Stock Photos

Beefed-up rails

The top and bottom layers of an iSUP board are held together on the sides by layers of PVC that form the rounded *rails* of the board (see Chapter 2). The shape of the PVC rails also creates the *rocker* line of the board — the banana-shaped, curved-up nose and tail of the board — when fully inflated. The rails often take the most punishment when you set down or drop the board, bang it with the paddle, or bump it into obstacles. For that reason, the rails usually have additional layers of PVC material to make them extra strong, which also adds rigidity.

REMEMBER Thermal welded rails hold up better over time than glued layers. Welded technology is generally more expensive but may be worth it in the long run.

The armor: PVC layers

You can think of the outer layer of your iSUP as armor, made of military-grade PVC. This material is tough enough to handle bumps and scrapes, and it can bounce off rocks without getting damaged. Most boards have multiple layers of PVC to make them even tougher. Impacts with blunt objects generally don't damage an inflatable board because it just bounces off (unlike a hard board, which isn't as flexible and is more likely to ding or crack).

WARNING Be careful around sharp, pointy objects, such as sharp rocks, nails, spikes, thorns, rusty metal with sharp edges, and so on, that can puncture the outer PVC layer. The good news is that small punctures in the outer skin are relatively easy to repair; check out the later section "Repairing your iSUP (because life happens)" for more on that job.

Keeping your inflatable happy

Maintaining your inflatable board is important. Here are a few maintenance tasks to help ensure your board's well-being.

Rinse before you repeat

A bit of sand, dirt, or saltwater residue won't necessarily damage your board as long as the metal parts (such as D-rings) are made of quality stainless steel. However, rinsing your board with fresh water after every use in salt water is still a good practice. If no fresh water is available — or if you roll the board up before it's completely dry — unroll it when you get home, rinse it with fresh water, and lay it out or hang it up to let it dry out.

If you roll up the deck pad and put it away wet, it can develop a coat of mildew. Getting rid of the musty smell resulting from that mildew can be very difficult.

Know when to let the air out

Transporting and storing your iSUP board while it's inflated is best for board longevity; rolling up the board creases and weakens the PVC over time. Make sure you don't store the board fully inflated, though; your best bet is to store it with less than five psi of pressure and then fully inflate it just before using it again.

Keep your cool (heat is the enemy)

Direct sunlight and overheating are the arch-nemeses of inflatable boards, so always store your iSUP in a cool, dark place, away from direct sunlight (that is, not in a sunny yard or hot attic or garage) if you want it to last for more than a few seasons. UV light and heat can damage and degrade the PVC material and glue, causing the material to weaken or become brittle over time. Freezing cold temperatures can also be a problem, but they aren't nearly as bad as heat.

When you're paddling a board on the water, heat generally isn't an issue, even on a very hot day, because the water underneath the board keeps it from overheating. On land, however, you have to be careful to avoid heat. If a board is fully inflated to the maximum recommended pressure in the shade or in cooler air temperatures but then left cooking in the sun on a hot day, the air inside can expand and the pressure increase dramatically. Keep a fully inflated board out of direct sunlight on a hot day, or at least remove some of the pressure when the board isn't in the water.

The sun's heat can also soften the glue holding the rail seams and PVC layers together, and the combination of higher pressure and weakened seams can cause the seams to burst open, which is very difficult to repair even for a pro.

Repairing your iSUP (because life happens)

Most iSUPs come with a repair kit (you didn't throw it away, right?) that includes a valve tool, PVC repair patches, and glue. You can see a sample kit in Figure 17-2.

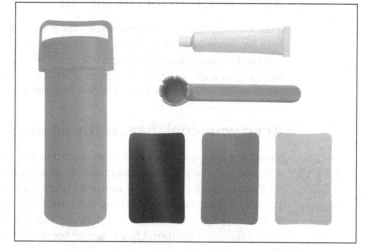

FIGURE 17-2:
A typical
iSUP
repair kit.

lilkin/Adobe Stock Photos

If you notice that the board is losing pressure, it isn't safe to use; you need to repair it promptly. To find the leak, fully inflate the board and listen for a hissing noise. If you can't hear anything, use a spray bottle with soapy water to find the puncture; even a slow leak should cause visible bubbling.

If the leak is around the valve, the repair may be as easy as tightening the valve by using the valve tool. Otherwise, follow these steps:

1. **Mark the leak with a marker and deflate and dry the board.**

2. **Place the board on a clean, level surface; put on rubber gloves and clean the area to be repaired with acetone to remove any dirt and oils.**

3. **Cut a patch 1 to 2 inches bigger than the puncture and pencil in an outline of the patch on the area of the board to be repaired.**

4. Apply painter's tape around the outline to keep the glue from getting all over the board.

5. Apply a thin, even layer of PVC glue to both the board and the patch, using a tongue depressor-type stick or a spatula.

6. Let the glue dry for about ten minutes until it feels dry to the touch.

7. Use a hair dryer or heat gun to gently heat up the glue on both the board and patch and then carefully align and apply the patch to the repair area.

8. Press the patch down firmly, making sure you force out any air bubbles.

9. Remove the painter's tape and place a heavy weight on the patch.

10. Allow 24 hours for the glue to dry and cure completely before inflating the board again.

Recognizing when to call an iSUP pro

DIY repair patches like those I discuss in the preceding section work for small punctures, but patching it yourself using the repair kit doesn't work in all situations. Take your board to a SUP professional if any of these occur:

>> The leak is along a seam.

>> The board has long tear.

>> The PVC layers are separating from each other, forming bubbles.

Some professionals can repair blown seams, but often that repair isn't worth it. At that point, all the seams on the board are most likely weakened, so even if you repair one issue, the board is likely to develop more leaks along the seams the next time you inflate it. Your best hope is to get a warranty replacement, which is why buying quality inflatables with a good warranty period (as I explain in Chapter 3) is important.

Peeking at What's under the Glass: The Anatomy of a Hard Board

REMEMBER

The construction methods used under a hard board's paint usually aren't visible when you look at boards in a shop. But they can make a big difference in a board's strength, weight, durability, and longevity, so understanding what you're getting for your money is important.

Knowing how a hard board is constructed can help you understand how to take care of your board — and maybe spark an interest in building one of your own one day.

The core

As I note in Chapter 3, most hard boards are made using a very lightweight foam core that's then covered by a tough outer shell to protect it. These cores are manufactured multiple ways:

» Computer shaped or molded

» Designed on a computer and then rough shaped by a shaping machine

» Shaped completely by hand (that is, old-school)

Here's how hand-shaping a board from a block of foam works:

1. The rocker line is cut out of a block of foam using rocker templates and a hot wire.

2. The outline of the board is marked on the bottom by using templates, as shown in Figure 17-3, and then cut out using a saw, as shown in Figure 17-4.

3. The board is then rough-shaped using a power planer, as shown in Figure 17-5, and finish-shaped using hand planer tools and sandpaper.

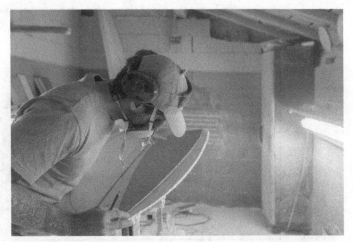

FIGURE 17-3:
Marking the boards outline using templates.

FIGURE 17-4:
Cutting the outline using a hand saw.

The tough stuff: Fiberglass and resin

The foam core blank (see the preceding section) is usually *laminated* (covered) with an outer shell consisting of fiberglass and resin. To optimize the weight-to-strength ratio, more advanced (and pricier) construction methods may include a thin layer of high-density PVC foam sandwiched between layers of fiberglass or other more high-performance woven materials such as carbon fiber (which is very stiff), Innegra, or Kevlar (very resilient).

FIGURE 17-5:
Using a power planer to shape the board.

Ideally, manufacturers use just enough (and no more) epoxy resin to fully saturate the woven materials. Additional resin adds weight but not strength. The resin is then cured, often in special temperature-controlled ovens, which hardens the outer layer into a tough shell.

Inserts

Inserts, such as *fin boxes* (which hold the fins), handles, and *leash plugs* (which secure your leash to the board) are installed into the board. You can read more about these parts in Chapter 2. On high-quality boards, the inserts are encased in stronger, high-density foam inserts and covered with additional fiberglass layers after installation.

Paint and finish

The final (and labor-intensive) step in hard board construction is smoothing out any imperfections, sanding, painting, finish-coating, and polishing the board before the deck pad is applied. Then a quality check usually occurs before the board is packaged and shipped.

Heeding Hard Board Maintenance and Repair

If performance is what you're after, a hard board is the obvious choice. Hard boards are more responsive, stiffer, and faster than inflatables, but they can also get damaged more easily from impacts. That's why you need to handle hard boards more carefully and maintain them well. If you take care of them properly, though, they have a longer life expectancy than inflatable boards and can last for decades. In this section, I cover hard board maintenance, care, and repair knowledge to help you keep your board in top shape so you can enjoy it for many years to come.

Maintaining a hard board

Here are some simple suggestions for maintaining your hard board SUP:

>> **Rinse your board with fresh water after using it in salt water.** That said, occasionally leaving a bit of salt water on the board doesn't necessarily damage your board, and you can easily wash off the resulting salt spots later.

>> **Clean the deck pad (see Chapter 2) with soap if it gets dirty or slippery.** Avoid using harsh chemicals on the board. A foam eraser cleaning sponge works well to clean boards with a dull sanded finish, but avoid using it on boards with a glossy finish; it can dull the coat.

TIP

I don't like to use surf wax because it tends to get dirty and messy, so I apply additional traction material if the included deck pad doesn't cover all the areas where I may place my feet.

Transporting and storing your hard board

In tropical locations like Hawaii, UV and heat can cause serious damage to hard boards, and heat combined with moisture inside a board is the most common reason boards age prematurely.

These issues usually crop up as a result of transportation and storage techniques.

Boards don't get hot while they're in the water because the water cools them down. Similarly, driving to and from the beach with a board strapped to the car isn't a problem because the moving air cools the board. But if you leave a hard board on or inside a parked car or on the beach in direct sunlight for long periods, the board can get very hot, and the heat can soften the epoxy resin that holds together the board.

Excess heat can also cause pressure to build up inside the board as the air expands. (This is especially true of dark-colored boards.) If the board has moisture trapped inside, the evaporating steam builds up even more pressure.

Over time, overheating can take its toll on hard boards, causing the surface to wrinkle, bubble, or *delaminate* (where the outer fiberglass shell separates from the foam). UV light also causes long-term damage such as faded colors and a decaying finish coat.

REMEMBER

Keeping the board in a bag helps prevent small scrapes and dings and protects it from UV light, but it doesn't necessarily protect it from heat. A padded board bag without ventilation can act as an oven, trapping heat and moisture inside. Ideally, you should store your hard board in a cool, shady location. If it must be outside in the sun (like in an outdoor surfboard rack), your best bet is to buy a white or light-colored board and store it in a thin, light-colored board sock such as the Lycra topless board cover shown in Figure 17-6.

Avoiding damage

Obviously, avoiding damage in the first place is best; an ounce of prevention is worth a pound of cure, right? The best way to do that is to handle your board carefully and store it away from potential threats. Be careful when you launch and come back to shore; beware of docks, rocks, and any other hard objects. Don't drag your board; avoid scratches by carrying your board into and out of the water.

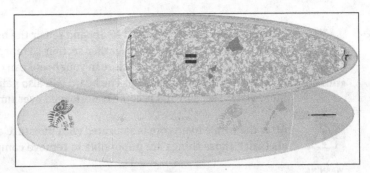

Some parts of the board are more prone to damage. Here are some tips for keeping those in good shape:

>> **Fins:** The fins are made to keep your board going straight in the water, not to hold up the board on land. Sideways and downward pressure on the fin can damage the fin box, which is an extensive repair. (So don't let your kids jump around on the board or put heavy things on top of it with the fin underneath it, either.) Remove the fins for travel, and package the board very well if you're shipping it.

>> **Rails:** The rails often take the most abuse, both from the paddler setting the board down on rough surfaces and from the paddle banging into the rails when you're paddling. Most of this damage is superficial and usually doesn't cause the board to leak, but I recommend applying clear protective rail tape to keep the rails looking good.

Dings happen: Repairing minor damage

If you paddle regularly, your board is going to get dinged. Whether you bang into another board or rocks while paddling or bump or drop the board accidentally while handling or storing it, dings are just part of the deal.

If a ding leaks water, you need to dry and repair the board before using it again. As I note in the earlier section "Transporting and storing your hard board," moisture in your board can cause problems when the board heats up. The board will also gain weight as more water seeps in and become waterlogged over time.

After the whole foam core is saturated with moisture and minerals (salt), those things are impossible to remove completely.

Being a ding detective

Regularly check your board for damage. Small surface scratches and dents that don't pierce the outer shell are usually fine to leave unrepaired if they don't allow water to get into the board. If you discover a crack or break in the fiberglass, or you see dried salt around a ding, it's time to take action.

UNDERSTANDING HOW WATER GETS INTO THE BOARD

The inside of most hard SUPs is made of expanded polystyrene (EPS) foam. Although different EPS foams have different qualities, all EPS foams have small gaps of air between the foam cells where water can seep in. The foam blank will take on water — some foams faster than others — if the outer shell is damaged. If you don't dry and repair a ding promptly, the water can accumulate and slowly spread deeper into the foam core.

When you take a board from a hot beach or car roof and put it into the cooler water, the air inside the board contracts. If your board has a self-venting plug, the plug slowly equalizes the pressure difference without allowing water to enter, but as that pressure equalizes, water can get sucked into the board quickly if your board has even a tiny leak. When the board warms up again, the opposite happens; the air inside the board expands, and water and air get pushed out of leaking dings. As the salt water evaporates, it can leave a telltale salty crust around the leak, so be on the lookout for dried salt around dings or inserts. It means you have a leak on your hands.

DIYing ding repair

Sealing small cracks and dings is easy and fast. Using a sticker or duct tape to cover the ding isn't recommended because these items usually don't form a good, watertight seal. My favorite method to seal small dings quickly is by using a two-part epoxy putty ding stick, which you can find at your local surf shop or hardware store.

These are the steps involved:

1. **Open the ding on your board enough so it can dry out completely.**

   Pushing the tip of a paper towel into the ding soaks up moisture and evaporates it more quickly.

REMEMBER

   You may need to wait several days for the ding to dry completely. If you put the tip of a paper towel in the crack and it still takes on moisture, you need to let it dry longer. You don't want to trap moisture under your repair.

2. **Rough up the area where you plan to apply the ding stick with sandpaper as shown in Figure 17-7.**

3. **Cut off a sufficient amount of the ding stick putty and thoroughly mix the two parts between your fingers until the colors are mixed together evenly and the putty has a chewing gum consistency.**

   Mixing the two different colored parts of the putty together activates the reaction and you have a limited time (about 5 minutes) to use and shape the mixed putty before it begins to harden.

   A little putty goes a long way.

4. **Shape and apply the putty to the ding as shown in Figure 17-8.**

   At this point, the putty will be sticking to your fingers as much as it's sticking to the board, so just roughly get it in place.

5. **Wash your hands well with soap to remove all putty residue and then use your wet hands to push the putty into the ding and shape/smooth it out.**

   The putty will stick to the board but not to your wet fingers, allowing you to smooth out the repair area as shown in Figure 17-9.

The thick consistency of the putty provides an instant seal, and you can take the board into the water as soon as the epoxy hardens — within about 30 minutes. If you sealed the ding properly, it will no longer take on water.

This process is a great way to quickly seal a ding so you can get back into the water. It isn't as permanent and strong as a professional repair and is more likely to crack if banged again in the same place, but as a stopgap measure it works just fine. For a more thorough home remedy, head to the following section.

FIGURE 17-7:
Rough up the area around the ding.

FIGURE 17-8:
Apply the repair putty.

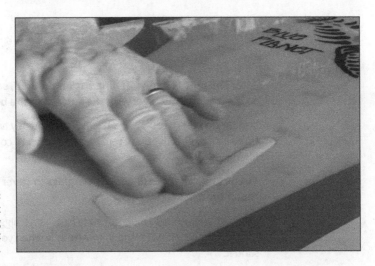

FIGURE 17-9:
Smooth out
the putting
using wet
fingers.

TIP

To watch a video where I use a ding stick to repair a crack, check out the one here: https://www.youtube.com/watch?v=Fg2mo3 vxJy0.

Making the repair more durable

Ding repair kits that improve upon ding sticks (see the preceding section) are available in most surf shops. These kits include some epoxy resin (UV curing is easiest to use) and fiberglass. Covering the repaired area with fiberglass and resin makes the repair more structurally solid and is the proper way to repair the board.

TIP

Make sure you get a kit that's suitable for epoxy repairs because polyester resin will melt the foam inside your epoxy SUP.

REMEMBER

The steps I spell out here assume that you've already done some heavy lifting by using a ding stick as I spell out in the previous section. What I'm proposing in the following steps is an "in addition to" and not an "instead of." The thick putty of your ding stick is what you need to completely seal the leak. If you only use the thinner resin and fiberglass technique here to cover the repair area, small pinholes can form while the resin is curing, and the board will continue to leak through the fiberglass. Sealing it with putty first is an important step.

Here's how to get a stronger bond than a ding-putty-only repair:

1. **After the putty from your ding stick has cured, sand it so it's smooth and level with the surface of the board.**

   Use sandpaper to rough up a bigger area (roughly two to three inches past the putty repair area) that you'll cover with fiberglass.

2. **Cut out two or three layers of fiberglass to cover the repair area.**

   Cutting the layers into different sizes (smaller to bigger) means your repair will blend in more easily when you sand it.

3. **Put masking tape around the repair area to keep resin from getting all over the board.**

4. **Wearing rubber gloves, lay the first layer of fiberglass over the ding and saturate it with resin by using a small brush or squeegee; then apply the second (and third) layer of glass.**

   If you're using UV curing resin, apply it indoors or in a shady place because it will quickly cure in direct sun.

TIP

5. **Expose the UV curing resin to the sun and wait for it to cure completely.**

   If you are using two-part epoxy resin, measure and mix part one and part two of the resin to activate the resin before applying as per the instructions. Two-part epoxy will only harden if the ratio of the two parts is exactly right, so make sure to measure the amount carefully.

6. **Once the resin is cured (hard), hand sand the repair until it's smooth and is blended in with the surface of the board.**

7. **Paint another smooth layer of resin (a sanding coat) over the repair and let it cure; then sand it smooth until it has no low spots or lumps.**

   Repeat with another sanding coat if necessary.

If the spirit moves you, you can apply a finish coat of resin, sand it with increasingly finer-grit sandpaper, and finally polish it to get a shiny finish. I usually don't have the patience for this step.

Knowing when to call a hard board pro

More involved repairs take additional steps and skills that go beyond the scope of this book, but I include some resources in Chapter 23 if you're interested in finding out about more complicated repair procedures. For most people, I don't recommend DIY repairs if any of the following are true:

>> The damage is on the rails or along the edges of the board, as shown in Figure 17-10.

>> The damage occurs over more than a few inches and/or goes deep into the foam of the board.

>> The damage is around fin boxes or other inserts.

>> The outer layer of the board has separated from the foam (delaminated).

>> You want the board to look as good as new, with perfectly matching colors. Only the best repair shops can do this.

FIGURE 17-10: Repairing the rails and sharp edges takes special skills.

Sunshine Seeds/Adobe Stock Photos

Chapter **18**

SUPer Adventures: Paddle Adventure Guide

I t may be a stab in the dark, but I'm going to assume that because you have my *For Dummies* book in your hands, chances are you're feeling the draw of stand up paddleboarding, and you can hear the world saying to you, "Come explore me!" Being outside in the sunshine, one with the water, and immersed in a beautiful landscape while paddling through some of the most stunning environments of the world — all that's very hard to resist. Whether you stay local or go halfway around the planet, planning a paddle getaway is exciting and gives you something to look forward to.

REMEMBER

Paddling is a great excuse to travel and to explore and experience some of the world's most beautiful places while being active and engaged. If you feel the need for some paddle adventure in your life, this chapter gives you some great ideas on where to start.

STICKING CLOSE TO HOME

One thing I learned during the COVID-19 pandemic is that you don't have to travel far to have an adventure. It's about experiencing something different and new. You probably still have many areas in your local waterways that you haven't explored yet. So instead of going on the same route every week, pull up a map and make a point of discovering some new places to paddle. The trick is to wait for the right conditions, maybe invite some friends, and just do it! A simple change of scenery makes paddling more exciting and enjoyable, and exploring new places makes getting outside and paddling feel more like an adventure.

For example, my friend Jeff Chang and I planned a paddle adventure here, around the island of Oahu. We waited for good conditions with light winds that would allow us to paddle around the coastline of the entire island. We had to stretch it out over several months, but we completed the route of 124 miles over three separate days. Along the way we encountered plenty of ocean life — including whales, dolphins, turtles, and sharks — as well as stunning scenery, sunrises, and sunsets. Coming around the remote Ka'ena Point nature reserve was one of my most rewarding and memorable experiences on a SUP. The following figure shows me paddling along the remote coastline around Ka'ena Point on Oahu's west side.

Setting out on Your Own Great Adventure

You can tackle countless places and water types on a SUP. In the following sections, I offer just a few ideas that can expand your horizons and offer rewarding experiences both closer to home and in faraway places.

Windy places for SUP downwinders

If you love downwinders (paddling in the direction of the wind), whether on a traditional SUP downwind board or a SUP foil board, gliding along with the wind and surfing on endless bumps is an incredible experience. Many places in the world offer reliably consistent, strong winds to create the wind swells ideal for downwinding.

REMEMBER

Although most waterways can sometimes experience favorable wind conditions for downwinding, the wind isn't always blowing *consistently* in most places. You need to watch the weather report and be ready to drop everything to go when conditions are favorable, which isn't always easy if you have a job.

TIP

If you're going on a vacation and have limited time available, your best bet is to choose a location that has a high probability of experiencing consistently good conditions. Some of the most popular destination locations around the world with consistent, strong winds for downwinders are these:

>> Maui's famous Maliko Run has some of the most consistent wind conditions in Hawaii. The unique shape of the island (they don't call it "Valley Isle" for nothing) causes the wind speed to increase as it gets funneled through the valley between the mountains.

>> The section of the Columbia River Gorge around Hood River, Oregon, has reliably strong wind. The thermal wind gets channeled through the gorge and blows against the river current, which creates steep swells that are relatively easy to catch and ride.

>> The coastal areas bordering the city of Cape Town, South Africa, are known for their abundance of strong, steady winds and great downwind runs, including the famous Millers Run.

>> Western Australia around Perth has famous downwind runs with epic conditions during its summer season (which is winter in the Northern Hemisphere).

>> Tarifa on the southern tip of Spain has strong winds that get channeled through the Strait of Gibraltar.

>> Lake Garda in Northern Italy has consistent thermal winds that funnel through the long, narrow lake, making it a European wind sport magnet.

REMEMBER

Although many more locations around the world are windy, popular locations like the ones I list here offer not only consistent wind conditions but also the option to rent boards, join a group, or attend a class; well-established launch and exit sites; the needed infrastructure; and lots of other wind sport enthusiasts.

The infinite variety of SUP surfing adventures

For a SUP surfing adventure, you want to go to a place that serves up consistently good wave conditions. Unfortunately, the most well-known surf breaks are often crowded, so finding good, uncrowded waves in remote locations that are off the beaten path can be a challenging but also very rewarding experience.

REMEMBER

Wave conditions vary by season, so do your research on when conditions are most favorable. For more on SUP surfing in general, check out Chapter 13.

Boat trips

For a different kind of SUP surfing adventure, you can try a boat-based trip. A boat trip involves using a boat as your home base to explore remote surf spots or surrounding islands. If you or a friend has access to a boat, you can plan your own boat trip adventure along almost any coast.

If budget isn't a concern, some of the most popular destinations for commercial SUP surfing boat trips are as follows:

>> **The Maldives:** These beautiful islands in the Indian Ocean (about 470 miles/750 kilometers southwest of Sri Lanka and India) have a smorgasbord of waves suitable for all levels.

>> **Indonesia:** I went on a SUP surf boat trip in the Mentawai Islands in Indonesia, where the boat motored to the next surf spot overnight and anchored before sunrise so we were able to explore a new surf spot every day. In addition to the Mentawai Islands, which are probably the most popular destination for boat trips, many other areas in Indonesia (the Banyak Islands, Sumba, Sumbawa, and Roti, for example) offer organized SUP surfing boat trips.

>> **Fiji:** You can only reach some of the best waves in Fiji by boat, but typically people stay at a land-based resort and take a boat to the surf breaks.

Dave Kalama's Kalama Kamp is a one-week, all-inclusive camp on Fiji's Namotu Island where he coaches SUP, surfing, and foiling skills. This camp usually sells out well in advance; for details, visit kalamakamp.com/.

Riding the longest waves in the world

If you want to SUP surf some of the longest-breaking waves on the planet, here are two spots known as some of the world's longest ridable waves:

>> **Chicama, Peru:** If you're lucky, you can ride for as long as 1.4 miles (2.2 kilometers).

>> **Pavones, Costa Rica:** This wave is a legendary left-hand point break in southern Costa Rica.

Riding novelty waves

Sure, you can find lots of different SUP locations in this great wide world, but far-flung locales aren't the only way to spice up your SUP life. You can also find novelty in the kinds of waves you end up surfing. I cover a couple of options in the following sections.

Tidal bores

Tidal bores are waves caused by an incoming tide that pushes upstream along rivers. One of the unique features of tidal bore waves is you can ride them for many miles. Tidal bores require careful timing and local knowledge; it may not sound exciting, but a successful ride can be unforgettable. Some of the most well-known locations with tidal bores are these:

>> The Bono Tidal Bore in Indonesia, known as the Bono Wave, is one of the tallest and longest tidal bores in the world, traveling up to 25 miles (40 kilometers) up the Kampar River.

>> The Pororoca breaks along the Amazon River in Brazil and is one of the longest and most powerful tidal bores. Ride one of its waves, and you can end up traveling up to 8 miles (13 kilometers) inland.

>> The Quintang River Tidal Bore in China is known as the Silver Dragon. It produces some of the tallest, fastest tidal waves in the world. *Note:* Its size and speed make it dangerous to ride, so it's better for more-advanced thrill-seekers.

>> The Petitcodiac River Tidal Bore in New Brunswick, Canada, stretches for several miles and is one of the top locations for tidal bore SUP surfing in North America.

>> The Severn Bore in England is a well-known bore in Europe and can offer long rides to SUP surfers.

REMEMBER

To ride a tidal bore, you need to research when the tide conditions are right to create a good tidal bore wave, make sure you're in the right place to catch the tidal bore, and arrange transportation if you ride the wave for miles. Having a support boat or personal watercraft is a good option because it can help you catch up with the wave if you fall in and give you a ride back to the starting point.

Tanker surfing

Big container ships, oil tankers, ferries, and other large ships passing through shipping channels can create big wakes that can break and be surfed along shallow banks. The weight, size, and speed of the ship and the bottom contours all have to work together to create ridable waves. The best quality waves occur where the tanker wakes go over a shallow ledge, so experience and local knowledge is helpful.

REMEMBER Never surf wakes close to a ship and don't obstruct shipping lanes.

Many ports around the world are suitable for surfing tanker waves. In Galveston, Texas, a company even specializes in tanker surf charters (tankersurfcharters.com/). As in tidal bore surfing (see the preceding section), a support boat or watercraft is very helpful in case you fall.

TIP Phone apps and websites, such as www.marinetraffic.com, allow you to track large ships to predict when these waves may occur.

SUP touring

Long-distance paddle tours can be same-day trips or multiday adventures through beautiful areas. Though some people enjoy the competitive spirit of long-distance adventure races like those I outline in Chapter 16 many paddlers simply want to enjoy the ride and experience the adventure without the added pressure of competitive racing.

Some people enjoy a social paddle that takes them to a destination with a café or restaurant; they stop to have lunch and then paddle back. Longer, multiday trips take more planning but allow you to explore more remote areas. One popular destination for multiday trips is the Boundary Waters Canoe Area in Minnesota, which features thousands of interconnected lakes. SUP touring allows you to experience this pristine wilderness while camping at designated campsites at night. Planning and packing light are essential because you may have to *portage* (carry) all your equipment from one lake to the next.

REMEMBER Before setting out on an overnight trip, find out whether permits and/or reservations are required. Most wilderness areas are protected and only allow a limited number of visitors at a time. For popular destinations, you often need to plan a year or more in advance to apply for the needed permits. If you're planning to rent gear from a local outfitter, they can usually help guide you through the planning and permitting process.

TIP

Race locations can be great candidates for leisure tours. I've competed in many races in beautiful places, including along the Na Pali coast race along Kauai's remote North Shore. Racing along this beautiful coastline is exhilarating, but I feel like I wasn't able to fully enjoy it during the race. I want to go back and paddle the Na Pali coast without time pressure, take plenty of stops along the way, and maybe even bring camping gear to stay overnight along the way. (Don't worry; I'll also bring a camping permit.)

River trips

Paddling down a river gives you a new perspective; you may encounter wildlife, rapids, canyons, and beautiful campsites as you go. Whether you're paddling down a slow-moving river, as in Figure 18-1, or charging down turbulent rapids, river trips are always memorable adventures.

The ultimate river trip is going through the Grand Canyon, although this expedition requires skill to make it through the challenging rapids. (If you bring an inflatable SUP along on a rafting trip, you can always choose to go in the raft if you aren't up to the challenge of going through the rapid on the SUP.) Other fantastic river trips include the Green River in Utah, the Sacramento River in California, the Colorado River, and many more.

FIGURE 18-1:
Paddling down a slow-moving river.

neiros/Adobe Stock Photos

Night paddling

If you're looking for a unique and extra-magical way to experience SUP, try paddling at night. Assuming the moonlight cooperates, you may be able to paddle without any lights. As your eyes adjust to the darkness, you can see light reflecting off the water surface, and the surreal peace and quiet of gliding through the darkness can be intoxicating.

You can also strap LEDs to the bottom of the board and paddle with a magical glow. At the Blue Planet Adventure Company in Haleiwa, we offer Glow Down the River SUP Tours, as shown in Figure 18-2, and Flow and Glow Yoga after sunset. For details, visit blueplanetadventure.com/local-activities/.

FIGURE 18-2: A turtle joins the Glow Down the River Tour in Hale'iwa.

LEARNING ON THE RUN

If you're looking to enhance your skills and are interested in teaching others, taking an instructor certification course or other class or clinic in a beautiful location can be a great learning experience and a fun adventure at the same time. SUP instructor training certifications

(continued)

(continued)

are offered in many places through programs from these organizations:

- Professional Stand Up Paddle Association (PSUPA; www.psupa.com/)
- World Paddle Association (WPA; worldpaddle association.com)
- American Canoe Association (ACA; americancanoe.org)
- International Surfing Association (ISA; isasurf.org/)

Clinics and group classes are another great way to meet other paddlers that share your interests, improve technique, find out about new places to paddle, and bolster your safety and confidence on the water. Countless SUP clinics and courses are offered all over the world.

Traveling the World to SUP: Challenges and Rewards

The rewards of traveling around the world to SUP are obvious: You get to have memorable experiences in some of the most beautiful places on the planet. The anticipation of going on an adventure as well as the journey itself and the unexpected things that happen along the way all make it even more interesting — but can also be challenging if you aren't prepared.

Dealing with luggage- checking guidelines

Traveling with a SUP can be challenging. If you're taking a small surf SUP, you may be able to check it in like regular luggage, but bigger hard boards are often too big to check on a plane. Most airlines limit the size of "surfboard" bags to around nine feet; many SUPs are longer than that, so make sure to check the airline baggage policy before booking a ticket if you plan to travel with a hard board. Keep in mind as well that many airlines calculate the size of the board bag by using linear dimensions (length plus width plus thickness), so make sure the sum of the three dimensions is smaller than the maximum allowed. The rules may vary depending on the route you're traveling and the type of aircraft.

TIP

When I travel with a board bag, I always try to use the curbside check-in service if it's available. The valets work for tips and not only help you haul your luggage and check it in for you but also are usually more helpful than the airline employees on checking in oversized luggage and bending the rules for you if necessary.

Most iSUPs are compact enough that you can check them as regular luggage, so they're much more convenient to travel with than hard boards. You can also carry an iSUP as a backpack, which allows you to take it to more remote waterways, such as alpine lakes that require a long hike to reach. Plus, you aren't as dependent on ground transportation and board storage at the destination.

Knowing when you should rent a board

Traveling with your own board has obvious advantages: You get to ride the performance board you're used to and don't have to make do with what's available. The transportation charges of bringing your own board may also cost less than renting, especially if you're paddling for more than a few days. In some cases, though, renting can be the best option:

>> If you prefer using a hard board, the hassle of transporting the board; getting it to and from the airport; storing and moving it around while you travel; packing, unpacking, and repacking it; and the risk of damaging your board during transit (not to mention the baggage fees) can make renting seem like a great value in comparison.

>> Local conditions may also require a different type of board than what you usually ride.

>> Even if your board is fine for the location, renting can give you the opportunity to try several different boards to see what works best for you in the conditions.

Reserving a rental board is a good idea if you're looking for more than the bulky, heavy, banged-up, super-stable beginner cruiser boards that most SUP rental locations have available. Many rental operations in popular SUP locations offer reservation service, so researching whether suitable rentals are available before you decide to travel with your own board is worth your time. For example, at Blue Planet (blueplanetadventure.com/), we offer not only our standard SUP rental boards but also premium SUP rentals, including high-performance SUP surfing and SUP racing boards, that can be reserved for multiday hires.

Making a travel list (and checking it twice)

Whether you're headed on a SUP surfing trip to Tahiti, participating in an inter-island SUP race, or going on a multiday river trip, putting together a checklist of all the items you need to pack can help you ensure you don't end up on a remote beach without the right tools to attach the fins to your board. (Don't ask how I came up with that example.) Here's the checklist I use:

- ≫ Board and paddle (these are obvious)
- ≫ Leash, fins, and related items (don't forget screws, tools, and leash string)
- ≫ Personal floatation device (PFD, which many locations require; flip to Chapter 5 for PFD options)
- ≫ Waterproof bags (for phone and gear)
- ≫ Wetsuit or drysuit (if necessary; I break down the differences in Chapter 6)
- ≫ Sun protection (hat, sunscreen, long-sleeved water shirt; see Chapter 6)
- ≫ Hydration pack and nutrition (you don't want to collapse because of lack of food or water)
- ≫ Dry clothes (and layers for different climates)
- ≫ First aid kit and medicine

>> Camping gear if applicable (tent, sleeping bag, mat, kitchen gear, food)

>> Satellite communication device (if you plan on being outside cellphone reception areas; see Chapter 5)

Joining organized tours versus planning your own adventure

When you're planning for a SUP adventure, one of the decisions you have to make is whether to join an organized tour or plan the trip yourself. Both approaches have their benefits and disadvantages.

Organized tours

Going on an organized SUP tour is ideal if you're new to the sport, want to be able to explore unfamiliar territory without the stress of logistics, or don't have a friend, partner, or group of people to plan the trip with. Aspects such as local transportation, accommodations, meals, and necessary equipment are included or planned out for you, so you can just show up and have fun with minimal planning or stress involved.

Organized trips are usually planned and led by experienced guides who have the local knowledge needed for off-the-beaten-path locations and once-in-a-lifetime experiences that you may not have access to otherwise. A good guide can also give you technique tips, make you aware of safety risks, and have contingency plans if things do go wrong, so traveling with an organized group is generally less risky than a DIY tour.

Self-planned tours

When you plan your own SUP adventure, you're in complete control of all the details of your trip. You can choose your destination (many destinations don't have organized trips available anyway), timeline, and pace. For example, group tours have to adjust the pace to the slowest person in the group, so you may not be able to paddle at your preferred pace.

Planning your own trip requires significantly more work and preparation, especially on the logistics side, but it also gives you the freedom to adjust your plans along the way. You can paddle and explore what interests you at your own pace on the equipment of your choice and according to your preferred schedule.

REMEMBER

You can usually save some money by doing the legwork yourself and by traveling during the off-season if that's an option for you. Research is important because you need to consider expected local weather conditions, including tides, winds, water and air temperature, and weather forecasts. You also need to study maps, read travel guides and blogs, and learn as much as possible about the destination.

TIP

Even if you plan your own adventure, hiring a local guide or instructor if available is often worthwhile to get some local knowledge and insights. When my family took a trip to Venice, Italy, for example, we hired a local guide (https://www.sup invenice.com/) to guide us on a SUP tour through the narrow canals. You can see me paddling under a Venetian bridge in Figure 18-3.

FIGURE 18-3: Your author paddling under a bridge in Venice.

Enjoying the Stand-Up Paddle Lifestyle

The SUP lifestyle isn't just about paddling; it's about embracing and finding joy in an adventurous, active, and nature-focused way of life. For many enthusiasts, SUP becomes more than just a hobby; it's a way to connect with nature, stay active and fit, meet like-minded folks, and explore the world. Here's to wanderlust and bucket-list SUP adventures, whether they're close to home, as for the Oregon-lake paddler in Figure 18-4, or take you halfway around the world.

FIGURE 18-4: Paddle adventure on a remote lake in Oregon.

micah/Adobe Stock Photos

The Part
of Tens

Consider all the relevant factors before you buy a board.

Find ways to up your paddling speed.

Watch out for and treat common injuries.

Enjoy SUP in a variety of interesting ways.

Get more info on lessons, certification, and the SUP community.

Chapter **19**

Ten Things to Ask Yourself Before Buying a Stand Up Paddleboard

uying a SUP can be a significant investment, so you need to understand — before you buy — what type of board will most likely work best for you. Finding the perfect board can feel overwhelming with so many choices available on the market today. Beginners often focus on the price and looks of the board, but many factors play into making an informed decision. Speaking from personal experience, I can tell you that we ask folks who come into our Blue Planet shops wanting to buy a board lots of questions to help them make an informed decision about the best possible fit between their wants and needs.

In this chapter, I offer ten key questions you should ask yourself before committing to a purchase. By thinking about these ten points, you're well on your way to making an informed purchase decision. Whether you're just starting out or upgrading to a more advanced board, taking the time to evaluate your needs and wants helps you choose the best stand up paddleboard for your paddling conditions, skills, lifestyle, and ambitions.

Will I Be Sharing My SUP Equipment?

If you plan to share the board with others, you want a versatile, stable, and durable beginner board that's suitable for the least skilled paddler.

TIP

For a board you're going to share with a partner or others, answer the questions in this chapter from the perspective of the lowest common denominator. If you're sharing the board with less-skilled paddlers, paddlers who weigh more than you do, or people who plan to paddle with a passenger or pet, you should answer the questions with those scenarios mind.

If you plan to share the board, a wide, higher-volume, durable, versatile all-round board is probably the best choice. (Flip to Chapter 3 for more on all-round boards.) A lightweight, specialized, tippy, expensive, high-performance board may be a perfect fit for you, but it isn't a good board to share with beginners.

As I mention in Chapter 4, the paddle is another very important piece of equipment. If you're sharing, a durable, adjustable paddle is the best choice. Otherwise, you can choose a lightweight, high-performance, fixed-length paddle that's sized just right for you.

REMEMBER

You aren't necessarily tied to this choice for life. We find at Blue Planet that many paddlers end up buying a stable, durable, inexpensive beginner board (and paddle) as their first. As they progress, they keep this board in their quiver to share with others while choosing a second board tailored to their specific needs for their exclusive use.

Do I Want an Inflatable SUP (iSUP) or a Hard Board?

The answer to this critical question depends on your lifestyle, storage space, transportation, and usage needs.

I compare the pros and cons of hard boards and iSUPs in Chapter 3. The main advantage of inflatable boards is that they're easier to transport and store than hard boards. They're also less likely to get damaged from blunt impacts. iSUPs can be ideal for entry-level paddlers in calm conditions. They're also great for sharing with others (see the preceding section). Just make sure you'll be able to store your iSUP in a cool place.

Hard boards generally offer better rigidity, responsiveness, speed, and glide. The rigidity may also make them feel more stable than an iSUP of similar dimensions. If you plan to get into SUP surfing (see Chapter 13) or racing (Chapter 12) or you put a premium on performance, hard boards are the best option. They do need more storage space and usually need to be strapped to a rack for transport. They can require more maintenance (which I outline in Chapter 17), but if you keep the shell watertight, hard boards have a long life expectancy.

TIP

In addition to answering this question academically, I recommend demoing a few inflatable and hard boards to see how they work for you in real life.

What Are My Height and Weight?

Your height and weight play a significant role in determining the appropriate SUP board size and volume for you, so this question is essential to ensure that you don't end up with a board that's too unstable or too sluggish for your size. A heavier, taller person requires a longer, wider board with more volume than a shorter, lighter person.

The volume and width of the board are especially important factors for choosing a board with adequate stability and buoyancy.

For larger paddlers, wider (more than 32 inches), longer (over 10 feet), higher-volume (over 200 liters) boards are recommended.

For a shorter, lighter person, a narrower (less than 32 inches), shorter (9-to-10 foot), lower-volume (up to 150 to 180 liters) board is easier to carry and transport and more maneuverable than a bigger board, though it should still provide enough stability to paddle comfortably.

What's My Skill Level?

Your experience level makes a difference, so be honest here. A common mistake paddlers make is overestimating their skills and buying a board that's too advanced for them. Beginners typically need more stability and volume, meaning a wider, higher-volume board with full rails (see Chapter 2).

As you progress, your balance improves, and you can comfortably paddle on a smaller, narrower board. Advanced paddlers may choose a longer, narrower board for more glide and speed, or a shorter, lower-volume board with thinner rails for maneuverability when surfing waves.

I always encourage paddlers to challenge themselves a bit, but you need to be realistic and move in small increments as you progress. I don't recommend going more than 6 inches shorter, more than one or two inches narrower, or more than 10 to 20 liters lower in volume when buying a new board.

REMEMBER

Being realistic about your skill level helps you pick a board that allows you to progress with confidence.

What Conditions Will I Be Paddling in Most Often?

Consider where and under what conditions you'll be using your board the most. The type of water and conditions — whether it's calm lakes, slow rivers, choppy bays, rough open seas, or surf — affects which board shape works best for you. Choosing a board designed for the conditions you usually paddle in will make it that much more enjoyable to use.

Here's a list of the kinds of boards best suited for different conditions; you can read more about many of these board types in Chapter 3:

>> **Flat water:** For calm lakes and smooth water, all-round or touring boards work best. Boards with less rocker (see Chapter 2) have a longer water line and generally glide and track better in calm water than boards with more rocker. For racing, narrow displacement hull boards with relatively low rocker are fastest in flat water.

>> **Choppy water or open ocean:** Pointy noses and narrower displacement hulls cut through chop more efficiently than the wide, flat noses usually found on all-round boards. A touring board or race board is most efficient if you plan to paddle for long distances. A bit more rocker than a flatwater board is helpful to navigate rougher water.

>> **Open ocean downwinding:** For downwinding in good conditions with 15 knots (about 17 miles per hour) or more wind, I prefer using a board with more rocker and a planing hull (flat bottom) because it creates more lift that lets the board slide over the water as you ride the swells. The extra rocker follows the contours of the ocean and keeps the nose from plowing into the trough in front of you.

>> **Waves:** For surfing, a shorter, narrower, lower-volume board is more maneuverable and allows for better performance on the wave. More rocker curve makes the board easier to turn on the curved face of the wave, while less rocker can make the board faster.

>> **Rivers:** If you plan to paddle on rivers with currents, rapids and eddies, consider a wider board that offers stability but also one that's relatively short so it's still easy to maneuver around tight corners. Durability is very important because you're more likely to bump into things.

What Are My Future Goals and Ambitions?

You may have goals to improve your skill level and to use your board in a more advanced way than you do your current board. Giving yourself a challenge by getting a board that's a bit more advanced than you are so you can grow into it is good. Just don't overdo it! You don't want to buy a board that you can't comfortably paddle — you'll get frustrated and won't use it — so be sure to take small, measured steps, not giant leaps.

To help you answer this question, here are some typical SUP goals and the kinds of boards that align well with them:

>> **Casual paddling:** A versatile, all-round SUP is a good option if you're using the board primarily for cruising and casual outings on flat water. As you progress, consider a more specialized board that challenges your balancing ability.

>> **Touring:** For longer trips and exploring open water, consider a slightly longer touring SUP that cuts through chop better and is more streamlined for better tracking, glide, and speed. As you progress, a narrower board will be faster but also more tippy.

>> **Racing:** It's all about speed, baby, so competitive paddlers use narrower, longer boards built for speed and performance. As you progress, you can try to use narrower boards. Head to Chapter 12 for details on SUP racing.

>> **Surfing:** When you're riding on the wave, a smaller board feels looser and easier to turn and fits into the *pocket* (the steepest, most powerful part of the wave) of the wave better. That said, smaller isn't always better: A shorter, smaller board is also more difficult to paddle back out on, and tiny boards are harder to catch waves on, especially in rough conditions. Some SUP surfers have gone back to using bigger, longer boards after going smaller and smaller and getting frustrated. As you progress, try using shorter, lower-volume boards, but take small steps. Chapter 13 has more on SUP surfing.

>> **Fitness:** For SUP yoga or fitness-type use, a wide, stable board is the best platform for holding challenging poses and maintaining balance. Features such as an extended deck pad; anchor attachment point on the nose; and attachment points for paddle, hydration, and snacks are helpful. As you progress, you can try more challenging poses.

Aligning your board choice with your goals and ambitions helps ensure you get the most out of the experience.

What's My Ideal Balance between Budget and Performance?

Making a hardboard both lightweight and durable requires advanced manufacturing techniques (such as high-density foam sandwich construction technology) and high-quality materials (such as carbon fiber). The advantage is that a lightweight board is easy to carry and performs well on the water. The downside is that this type of construction is expensive, therefore weight, quality, and cost are closely linked.

The same goes for inflatable boards, higher quality heat fused layers and seams are lighter, more durable, and perform better, but also cost more. Basically, you get what you pay for.

>> **Budget:** If you're just starting out, a durable, heavier (but more affordable) board may be sufficient for your needs.

>> **Performance:** If you're committed to the sport and are looking for high performance, investing in a lighter, higher-quality option may be worth the added cost for you. Avoid boards that are light but very fragile, though; they're not worth the hassle.

Ultimately, finding a good balance between performance (weight and durability) and price is the name of the game when you're looking for a board that meets your needs without busting your budget.

Where Should I Buy My SUP?

Deciding where to buy can make a big difference in overall experience and satisfaction. Consider the following options:

>> **Specialty retailer:** Buying from a good specialty retailer, especially a local one, often results in the best overall experience, value, and satisfaction. A retailer who specializes in selling SUPs can provide you with guidance and expertise. Buying locally may also give you the valuable opportunity to test boards before purchasing, which can save you from buying a board that isn't right for you. If you have any warranty or service issues in the future, a local dealer can help you navigate and resolve those. (Check out the following section for more on considering the warranty.)

>> **Online retailers:** Online shopping is convenient; you can read the reviews from other buyers, and, if you're lucky, you may find a great deal. But buyer beware: Some "great" online deals turn out not to be so great when what you get isn't at all like what was advertised. Make sure you buy from reputable retailers with good warranty policies.

TIP

I don't recommend ordering an inflatable SUP package from Amazon because the return window is usually only 90 days. If the seams blow out after four months, you're out of luck.

>> **Big-box stores:** You may be tempted by a low-priced SUP package at a big-box dealer such as Costco. This one-size-fits-all package may be a good choice for getting started at a good price if you're willing to make do with the performance and quality of the available package. An advantage is that big-box stores often have generous return policies, so if it's not right for you or if it fails, you may well be able to take it back for a refund.

>> **Secondhand:** If you're on a budget, consider buying used. Just like new cars lose a lot of value when you drive them off the lot, new SUPs lose a lot of value the first time they hit the water. You may be able to find a good deal if

someone needs to get rid of their board. Carefully inspect the board for damage, wear, or soft spots before committing and beware of water intrusion issues that aren't easy to see. I talk about buying used boards in Chapter 3.

REMEMBER

The right place to buy depends on your budget, what you're looking for, your comfort level, and whether you have access to a good local shop.

What Kind of Warranty Does the Board Come With?

A good warranty policy provides reassurance, especially when you're purchasing a more expensive board. Most quality boards come with a one-year warranty, although some boards may have even longer ones. Whatever warranty you get, make sure you understand the terms. Most warranties cover manufacturing defects, not regular wear and tear, dings, or damage resulting from impacts or accidents.

TIP

A reliable warranty policy and good brand reputation means that the brand stands behind its product quality, and this peace of mind is worth paying a bit more for.

How Invested Am I in a Particular Model or Color?

TIP

Don't buy a board just for looks; what really matters is the performance on the water.

For many people, though, aesthetics is important. Many manufacturers offer several color and construction options of the same model. These may not always be in stock, so if you're set on a certain model, color, and construction, you may have to be willing to pre-order it and have the patience to wait for it.

Custom boards give you the freedom to not only order the exact dimensions you want but also specify the design and colors. You don't know exactly what a board will look like until it's done, though, and sometimes people are disappointed if the board doesn't look exactly as imagined. Custom boards can also take months to complete, so you have to be patient. Really, I recommend custom boards only for advanced paddlers who know exactly what they want.

Chapter **20**

Ten (Plus One) Tips to Go Faster

E very paddler has their own unique style and paddle technique. Some are more upright, bend forward more, use their arms more, reach farther forward, have a different cadence, or bend at the knees with every stroke. I can often recognize a paddler in the distance from their technique before I can recognize their features.

Starting with a Good Catch

You can apply power in many ways, but the one key ingredient that everyone who teaches paddle technique agrees on is that a good catch is essential. As I explain in Chapter 11, getting a good *catch* (paddle entry) is arguably the most important part of the stroke because it sets you up for success. A good catch means fully planting the blade into the water before applying power to the stroke.

If you start to pull on the paddle too early, as the blade is still splashing into the water, air gets pulled down and the blade slips through the water with less traction. Instead, reach forward and fully insert the blade from the side and/or straight down, planting it into the water until only the shaft is showing before you apply power. Turbulence from the blade edges creates air pockets that get pulled down into the water, as you can see in Figure 20-1. This turbulence creates slippage, reducing the efficiency and effectiveness of the stroke. Minimizing these air pockets maximizes the traction of the paddle.

FIGURE 20-1: Turbulence around the blade edges.

Powering up Your Stroke

The *power phase* of the stroke (see Chapter 11) is where you accelerate the board forward. The amount of power you apply is important, but so is the stroke rate or cadence. You may think that a bigger blade allows you to take more powerful strokes, but I've found that using a smaller blade with a slightly quicker cadence and good technique can result in higher average board speeds and less fatigue over longer distances.

TIP

A common beginner mistake is to use mostly the arms to paddle and to not engage other muscle groups enough. To make the stroke more powerful and efficient, work on using your arms less by keeping them relatively straight. Involve your whole body by twisting your torso to engage your lateral muscles, pushing down with your top hand, engaging your core, and using gravity to lean your body weight into the stroke. Bring your hips forward at the end of the power phase to straighten your upper body. Avoid pulling the paddle past your feet and keep a quick, fluid pace.

Make a Smooth Exit and Recovery

Wasted energy is what slows paddlers down. To improve your speed, you need to adopt the path of least resistance. That means making your blade entries and exits as smooth as possible.

Work on feathering (see Chapter 11) the blade so it comes out smoothly close to your feet. As you end your power phase, use a twisting motion of your top hand (pointing the thumb forward) to feather the *power face* (the side compressing the water) of the blade away from your body as you lift the paddle up with your bottom arm and move the blade back forward into the recovery phase (see the following section).

Working on Recovery

A clean exit allows the blade to slip out of the water smoothly and move back into the catch position quickly and almost effort-lessly, giving you a chance to relax, inhale, and reset for another clean catch and powerful stroke. This respite is the *recovery* phase, which I cover in Chapter 11.

REMEMBER

Your board accelerates forward during the power phase and decelerates during the recovery phase. Keeping the recovery quick and fluid and maximizing the amount of time the blade is in the water propelling the board forward lead to faster speeds. This concept is especially important when you're going into a headwind.

Minimizing Splashing

A good way to work on the efficiency of your stroke is to listen carefully. On a calm, quiet day, pay attention to the sounds of your stroke. Does each stroke sound like a bomb going off in the water?

If you notice a lot of water splashing and air gurgling, focus on getting a cleaner catch; work on slicing the blade into the water smoothly rather than splashing it down. You want to go into stealth mode: Make sure to plant the whole blade and then "surprise" the water with a quick and powerful stroke. The speed of the blade should match the speed of the board moving past the planted blade. If you're throwing water behind you or have a splashy exit, focus on ending the power phase by your feet, feathering (see Chapter 11), and getting a smooth, clean, efficient exit with minimal splashing.

REMEMBER

You know your stroke is smooth and efficient if all you can hear is the board slicing through the water and your strokes are quiet yet powerful.

Maximizing Leverage

Beginners often hold the paddle with their hands too close together. You get better leverage if your bottom hand is closer to the blade. You can achieve this position by widening your grip width, shortening the paddle, or both. Make a *paddler's box* by placing the paddle on top of your head and then making right angles with your elbows (with one hand on the shaft and one on the handle, as shown in Figure 20-2).

TIP

You can mark the lower hand placement on your paddle shaft with a piece of colored electrical tape to indicate roughly where that hand goes for better leverage when you paddle.

Stacking Your Shoulders to Improve Shaft Angle

Keeping the shaft vertical to the water is important for projecting yourself forward by using your paddle. Let me use a pole vaulter as an analogy. The pole has to be vertical to the ground for the vaulter to project themselves up as high as possible. Otherwise, they get catapulted sideways at an angle and don't go as high. The same is true when you're paddling; holding the paddle at a diagonal angle results in more turning of the board and less forward propulsion.

For the paddle to be vertical to the water, your top hand must reach out over the opposite rail. To get into this position, stack your shoulders and use your hips to balance out, keeping your center of gravity over the center of the board, as shown in Figure 20-3.

FIGURE 20-3: Stacking the shoulders.

stacked shoulders

Hips keep center of gravity over the board

Top hand over opposite rail

Paddle is vertical to water

Perfecting Your Blade Angle and Stroke Path

The stroke path and blade angle work together to control the direction of the board. If you find the board turning too much with every stroke, try starting the stroke a bit farther out away from the rail with the blade angled slightly inward and pull the paddle inward, toward you, ending close to the rail. You should always keep the blade at a 90-degree angle to the stroke path. By controlling the direction of the board, you can get more strokes per side before switching.

Getting into the Rhythm

After you get the board up to speed, you want to find a good rhythm — a stroke cadence you can maintain over the length of the course. If you're sprinting over a short distance, this pace can be close to 100 percent effort; for longer distances, you can shoot for around 80 percent of your maximum pace. I try to match my breathing to my stroke rate and count the numbers of strokes per side, focusing on smooth, efficient technique.

REMEMBER

On a longer board, you should be able to get at least six strokes per side before switching. Work on switching sides smoothly and quickly to keep up the board speed.

REMEMBER

To maintain a high paddle speed over long distances, endurance is key. Build your top speed with interval training and your endurance by increasing the training distance in small increments of no more than 10 percent per week.

Keeping an Even Keel

To maximize your speed, find a board that has a good balance of low drag and glide but with enough stability to allow you to paddle at full power without being too wobbly. Narrower boards have less drag, but if a board is too tippy for you and you need to constantly brace yourself with your paddle, you aren't able to put maximum power into each stroke. Most boards go faster if you keep them relatively level to the water surface.

Mind over Matter: Holding Your Emotions in Check

Keeping an even keel applies not only to your board (see the preceding section) but also to your emotional state, especially in SUP racing. Try to pace both your stroke rate and your emotions and focus on going the distance physically and mentally. You don't want to get too excited if you're doing well early on in a race, for example, only to hit a wall and flame out before the finish. Even casual paddlers can benefit from letting themselves get into this kind of zone.

TIP

Take some deep breaths and stay calm at the beginning of a paddle or race, set a pace you can maintain over the whole session, and focus on doing the best you can, not on what everyone around you is doing.

Conclusion

Mastering the art of paddling faster is about honing technique, maximizing efficiency, and maintaining both physical and mental endurance. Remember that it's not just about strength but also leveraging your body mechanics for maximum efficiency and propulsion. With practice and focus on these ten key tips, you will find yourself moving faster, smoother, and more confidently on the water.

Chapter **21**

Ten Ways to Deal with (or Prevent) Injuries

SUP requires a lot of repetitive movements, so as you get more serious about SUP and spend more and more time on the water, the risk of a repetitive strain injury increases. Injuries can take weeks or months to recover from, but with the right training, stretching, and recovery strategies, you can minimize the risk. In this chapter, I explore ten tricks that have helped me tackle — or outright avoid — common injuries to keep paddling strong all year long.

I'm not a doctor and am only speaking from my personal experiences.

REMEMBER

Relieving Common Injuries with Easy Exercises

As you paddle, you rely heavily on your shoulders, arms, core, back, hips, and leg muscles. The asymmetrical nature of some of the movements of these muscle groups can lead to overuse injuries if you don't balance the strength and flexibility of these particular muscles. Having a strategy for preventing and/or treating the injuries you're most likely to encounter.

As part of that strategy, I want to point out some of the most common overuse issues affecting SUPers and spell out some of the techniques that have helped me prevent and treat these problems:

>> **Shoulder injuries:** The repetitive motion of paddling and overuse can cause *shoulder impingement syndrome,* where the *bursa* (the fluid-filled sacs located between bones and muscles, tendons, or other soft tissue) get inflamed and swollen. If lifting your arm between 60 and 120 degrees as shown in Figure 21-1 causes a sharp pain at the top of your shoulder, you may have this injury. Rather than ignoring it (it'll only get worse), consider trying the following:

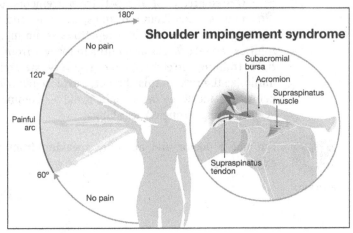

FIGURE 21-1: Testing for shoulder impingement syndrome.

Axel Kock/Adobe Stock Photos

- Rest helps treat this injury, but ultimately you need to strengthen the small rotator cuff muscles around your shoulder to strengthen the shoulders and protect them from reinjury.

  External rotation physical therapy exercises are important for paddlers because they balance out the pushing motion of paddling. I do lateral shoulder raises with an elastic band (see Figure 21-2) every morning and have found that this habit has kept my shoulders strong and injury-free.

- Using a shorter paddle with a smaller blade and softer shaft can help reduce the strain on your shoulder. Using good technique and always keeping your elbows below your shoulders while paddling can also help prevent this issue. For details on good paddling technique, flip to Chapter 11.

FIGURE 21-2: A simple lateral shoulder raise exercise.

lioputra/Adobe Stock Photos

>> **Tennis elbow:** Figure 21-3 illustrates another common overuse injury: inflammation of the tendon on the outside of the elbow (also known as *tennis elbow*).

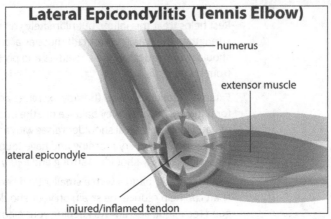

FIGURE 21-3:
Tennis
elbow.

Lateral Epicondylitis (Tennis Elbow)

humerus

extensor muscle

lateral epicondyle

injured/inflamed tendon

blueringmedia/Adobe Stock Photos

I had tennis elbow, and what worked best for me was strengthening my forearm muscles by using a Thera-Band flexbar and doing the Tyler Twist exercise. (A super-short YouTube video at www.youtube.com/watch?v=gsKGbq A9aNo demonstrates the Tyler Twist.)

>> **Lower-back pain:** Lower-back pain in paddlers can be caused by poor technique (paddling in a hunched forward position and not straightening back during recovery), having tight surrounding muscles (especially hips, hamstrings, and IT bands), and by increasing your training load too quickly. You can try to use a longer paddle and avoid excessively bending forward into each stroke to give your lower back a break.

I've found that hanging from a pull-up bar works well to relieve and prevent lower-back pain. I've also had success with these exercises (shown in Figure 21-4):

- Bird dog

- Thoracic extension stretch

- Standing hamstring stretch

- Cat-cow stretch

- Back extension

- Knee-to-chest stretch

- Swimming

EXERCISES TO RELIEVE BACK PAIN

① BIRD DOG

② THORACIC EXTENSON STRETCH

③ STANDING HAMSTRING STRETCH

④ CAT-COW STRETCH

⑤ BACK EXTENSION

⑥ KNEE TO CHEST STRETCH

⑦ SWIMMING

FIGURE 21-4: Exercises for preventing and/or relieving back pain.

inspiring.team/Adobe Stock Photos

WARNING

Although rest helps heal overuse injuries, strengthening the surrounding muscles before you get back into paddling is critical to prevent reinjury.

REMEMBER

These exercises have worked well for me, but if you're in pain, you should see a doctor specializing in these types of injuries and work with a physical therapist for guidance and treatment.

Strength Training

A strength training program is essential if you want to maintain a balanced physique and prevent injury. Building functional strength (see Chapter 14) in your core, legs, and upper body through varied exercises can increase your power and give you better control on the board. Here are some ideas to consider:

>> **Varying your exercises:** Don't focus only on the muscles used for paddling. That means you should try to integrate exercises that target the full body. Developing strength evenly results in a balanced physique that helps with good posture and technique and decreased injury risk.

>> **Making core strength "first among equals":** In Chapter 14, I explain how core strength is essential for SUP. But it also helps prevent injury. Paddling strengthens your core, and so do exercises such as planks, leg raises, and twists.

>> **Training fast-twitch muscle fibers:** Your muscle groups are made up of two kinds of muscle fibers: fast-twitch muscle fibers and slow-twitch muscle fibers.

Fast-twitch muscle fibers are responsible for quick, explosive movements; they contract rapidly but fatigue quickly. They're important for quick acceleration and sprinting short distances but aren't as useful for longer efforts. Lifting heavy weights for a few reps and doing short, high-intensity sprints activate fast-twitch muscles. (See the next bullet for the skinny on slow-twitch muscle fibers.)

>> **Training slow-twitch muscle fibers:** *Slow-twitch muscle fibers* contract more slowly and generate less force than fast-twitch muscles do, but they're highly resistant to fatigue, so they're essential for long-distance endurance paddling. High-rep, low-weight exercises target slow-twitch muscles, as does long-distance paddling.

Staying Limber: Flexibility and Mobility

Strength training (see the preceding section) bulks up your muscles, but it can lead to tightness, poor movement patterns, and eventually injury if the muscles aren't flexible and limber. Stretching and mobility work ensure that your muscles, tendons, and joints stay flexible and responsive. Focus on two distinct kinds of stretching:

>> **Dynamic stretching:** Before you hit the water, warming up and loosening your muscles with some *dynamic* (movement-based) stretches such as torso rotations, arm swings, jumping jacks, leg kicks, and the like is a good idea.

> » **Static stretching:** After paddling, you want to lengthen
> your muscles with *static* (stationary) stretches while your
> muscles are still warm, which can help you avoid muscle
> tightness later. Pay particular attention to your shoulders,
> back, hips, and hamstrings and hold each position for
> around 30 seconds.

Morning Routine: Starting the Day the Right Way

Developing a daily routine of stretches, mobility exercises, and strengthening exercises is a great way to keep your body limber and prepared for the demands of stand up paddleboarding. I've developed a routine of stretches, yoga poses, and push-ups that only takes about five to ten minutes, and I've made a habit of doing it every morning before I have coffee.

For a video of my morning routine, check out my YouTube video at www.youtube.com/watch?v=GJHPMMSik5w.

Fueling Yourself for Optimal Performance

Proper nutrition plays a key role in staying healthy and preventing injury. What you eat and drink powers your muscles, helps with recovery, and reduces inflammation:

> » **Balanced diet:** A mix of lean protein, complex carbohy-
> drates, and healthy fats provides sustained energy for
> paddling and for muscle recovery. Non-processed, nutrient-
> dense foods such as leafy greens, berries, nuts, lean meats,
> and whole grains should be staples of your diet. I love
> sweets, but I try to avoid refined sugar, opting to eat
> fruits instead.

>> **Hydration:** Staying hydrated is crucial in preventing muscle cramps and reduced performance. Drink lots of water before, during, and after your paddle sessions; adding electrolytes to the water can also prevent cramping.

Staying in Shape Year-Round

Maintaining a consistent level of fitness throughout the year is one of the best ways to prevent injury. As I explain in Chapter 12, downtime is important, but you don't want to let your fitness slide too much during the off-season. When you do, getting back in shape takes longer, and pushing yourself too hard too fast can lead to injury.

REMEMBER

Incorporating other sports into your fitness program (*cross-training* is the buzzword for that concept these days) can keep things more interesting and give your paddle muscles a break while working other muscle groups and keeping your cardiovascular system strong. Head to Chapter 12 for more on cross-training.

Recognizing the Importance of Rest and Recovery

The harder you train, the more you need to rest. Overtraining without adequate recovery can lead to chronic fatigue and increases the risk of overuse injuries. Here's what recovery should look like:

>> **Active recovery:** Here, you want to incorporate low-intensity activities like yoga, walking, or swimming at a light pace into your rest days. These activities keep you moving without putting too much strain on your muscles.

>> **Sleep:** Getting seven to nine hours of sleep each night gives your muscles time to fully recover and rebuild so you can go hard on your next paddle session.

Bringing in Breathing Exercises and Contrast Therapy

I'm a fan of Wim Hof breathing exercises to increase oxygen flow to the muscles, improve endurance and focus, and reduce stress. I cover the basics of the Wim Hof method (and other breathing exercises) in Chapter 7, but you can also check out a Wim Hof tutorial on YouTube at www.youtube.com/watch?v=nzCaZQqAs9I.

Contrast therapy (alternating between sauna sessions and cold plunges) works well to reduce muscle soreness, reduce inflammation, and speed up muscle recovery time.

Pacing Yourself: Avoid Overdoing It

Pushing yourself too hard or doing too much without proper preparation when you're just starting out or returning from a break often leads to injury. Taking a gradual approach is important; start with an easy pace and distance, allowing your body to rebuild endurance, strength, and flexibility over time.

REMEMBER

Taking small steps is the order of the day: Give yourself time to gradually increase the intensity, duration, and distance. My recommendation is to add no more than 10 percent distance per week if you're training for distance paddling or to slowly increase the pace if you're training for a shorter distance.

Making a Training Plan

Having a training plan can help you stick to a structured routine and build strength, endurance, and skills over time and without overtraining. Make the plan realistic, with gradual increases to avoid injury or burnout, and give yourself plenty of time to recover. For a sample distance–race training plan, see the nearby "My Molokai Race Training Plan" sidebar. I also cover training plans in Chapter 12.

REMEMBER

Many fitness apps are available to track your progress, and you can also keep a written journal of your progress. I have a Garmin GPS watch that syncs with the Garmin Connect app and lets me track time, distance, speed, and heart rate while also tracking the course. I also use an app called Elite HRV to track heart rate variability.

TIP

Tools such as Google Earth can help you map training routes. You can measure the length of a training run by using the Ruler tool and familiarize yourself with the course and landmarks from the satellite images. Use websites or apps to track the wind, wave, and tide conditions (I offer resources for doing that in Chapter 7) and note how they affect your times.

MY MOLOKAI RACE TRAINING PLAN

Training for the 32-mile Molokai to Oahu Paddleboard World Championships (M2O) for 15+ years has provided me with motivation to get in shape for this race (usually held at the end of July).

As I mention throughout the chapter, I try to stay in shape year-round with long, slow distance paddles, a morning routine, cross-training, and recovery. In the lead-up to the race, however, I use a more targeted plan, which I outline here.

Note: This sample 16-week plan assumes I'm already in good shape and a skilled paddler. You can vary it based on your level and needs.

Weeks 1 through 4: Building a base (with a focus on technique)

- **Two or three weekly paddles:** Long, slow distance (60 to 90 minutes); low-intensity (60 to 70 percent effort); focusing on smooth, efficient technique; increasing distance by no more than 10 percent per week. On Oahu, the Hawaii Kai to Kaimana downwind run is a good distance for this.

- **Cross-training:** One strength training and one interval training session per week.

- **Recovery day:** Take a day off from training with only light activity.

Weeks 5 through 8: Increasing endurance and strength

- **Three weekly paddles:**

- **Long paddle:** Increasing duration to two to three hours and 12 to 18 miles at a steady pace. On Oahu, I slowly increase the distance of the long downwind run by starting at Sandy Beach; finishing at Ala Moana or Sand Island; or going from Turtle Bay to Mokuleia on the North Shore.

- **Interval paddle:** 90 minutes of interval work alternating 5 minutes of hard effort (80 to 90 percent effort) and 5 minutes of easy effort (less than 50 percent of maximum effort).

- **Technique paddle:** 60 minutes focusing on technique, drills, balancing in rough conditions, and riding bumps.

- **One or two strength and conditioning sessions.**

- **One recovery day.**

Weeks 9 through 11: Race-specific preparation

- **Very long paddle:** Gradually increasing my distance until I'm close to the actual race distance (20 to 30 miles); training in similar conditions to Ka'iwi Channel; incorporating race day nutrition and hydration strategies to simulate the race. On Oahu, a good very long training run is Hawaii Kai to White Plains (21 miles), as shown in the nearby figure.

- **Tempo paddle:** 1.5 hours at race pace (75 to 85 percent effort).

- **Recovery paddle:** 60 to 90 minutes at slow pace to loosen up and work on technique.

- **Conditioning:** Focusing on core, stability, balance training, stretching, and injury prevention.

- **Rest and recovery:** Getting plenty of sleep and rest; contrast therapy.

(continued)

(continued)

Weeks 12 through 16: Taper and recovery

Doing the longest (close to race distance) paddle three to four weeks before the actual race to give my body plenty of time to recover. The last three weeks before the race, I decrease the training distance and focus more on technique and speed training as well as on rest, recovery, and breathing exercises.

Chapter **22**

Ten Ways to Enjoy SUP

SUP is one of the most versatile watersports, offering many different disciplines that can keep things fresh and interesting as your skills improve and you're ready to discover new ways to experience the sport. Yes, I do cover SUP racing in Chapter 12 and SUP surfing in Chapter 13, and they're as enjoyable as all get-out. But you have many other ways to enjoy stand up paddleboarding, which is why I ended up writing this chapter.

Most of the disciplines I list here easily deserve their own chapter (or book), but because of the limited scope of this particular tome, I can provide only a brief overview of some of the most popular and exciting disciplines to make you aware of the many things you can do on a stand up paddleboard.

SUP Touring

SUP touring combines the joy of paddling longer distances with the excitement of exploration and adventure. It's popular with adventure-seekers who love the idea of exploring new environments, embarking on multiday trips, experiencing nature up close, and testing their endurance. Touring boards are designed to glide and track well while offering more stability and storage options than a typical SUP race board. Attachment points allow you to transport food, water, safety gear, fishing equipment, and even camping gear for overnight trips.

REMEMBER

Touring boards are generally longer and narrower than your typical all-round SUP board and usually have less *rocker* (nose-to-tail curve) and more of a displacement shape (see Chapter 2), which allows them go faster and straighter while providing more stability and volume than a typical SUP race board. These modifications make them ideal for packing equipment for your adventure and for paddling longer distances at a steady pace.

TIP

If you're venturing out for long paddles in less-populated areas, make sure to go with a partner and to bring a communication device. (See Chapter 5 for your communication options.) A communication device that uses a satellite network is ideal because you may go out of range of a cellphone network.

SUP Yoga

Yoga enthusiasts have embraced the challenge of practicing yoga while maintaining balance on the water. Whether you're a seasoned yogi or a beginner, practicing yoga on a SUP is an excellent way to deepen your practice as you connect with nature.

Performing yoga on a SUP adds an extra layer of difficulty, focus, and mindfulness because the fluidity of the water makes poses more challenging and rewarding. The movements of the board on the water surface require exact weight placement on the board, subtle balancing adjustments, and greater core engagement than yoga on land. Even if you aren't into yoga, seeing whether you can balance on one foot (or even do a headstand on your board, as shown in Figure 22-1) is fun.

FIGURE 22-1:
SUP yoga
headstand.

SUP yoga boards are typically wider for added stability and have a longer *deck pad* (which provides traction and padding) to allow for those poses, such as downward dog, that require more space than a traditional deck pad offers. Boards are usually anchored to avoid drifting off during the yoga flow. The anchor can be a small weight or kayak anchor attached to a rope, which should be attached to the nose of the board. Calm, protected waters are ideal because they remove the added challenge of wind and choppy waves.

TIP

To maintain your balance, focus your gaze on something steady on land or on the horizon. Avoid looking down at the board and the water surface as they move around, which can make balancing more of a challenge.

REMEMBER

Some SUP yoga classes are even held in pools — and indoor pools make year-round classes possible, even in cold climates. If you're practicing SUP yoga in a pool, be sure to keep at least six feet of distance from the pool's edges to avoid possible injuries if you lose your balance.

SUP Fishing

For those who enjoy fishing, SUP offers a quiet and flexible alternative to traditional fishing boats or kayaks. Fishing from a SUP offers a variety of advantages:

>> The higher vantage point allows a better view into the water with less glare than you'd get in a sitting position (like in a kayak) so you can see fish more easily.

>> You can get closer to the fish in shallow waters and hard-to-reach fishing spots, all while enjoying the peaceful environment and getting a full body workout.

>> You have increased mobility and stealthiness, allowing you to sneak up on fish quietly without disturbing them.

SUP fishing boards are generally wider and more stable with thicker, full rails (see Chapter 2) to allow casting and fishing in a standing position. Even if you're comfortable paddling a narrower board, remember that the board is more tippy when it isn't moving, so this extra width and stability is important if you plan to fish in a standing position. Sitting on your board lowers your center of gravity and is a good option if the board isn't stable enough to fish in a standing position.

REMEMBER

Specialized SUP fishing boards are available that offer multiple attachment points for fishing gear, such as rod holders, tackle boxes, coolers, and so on. Some fishing SUPs also offer built-in storage compartments and seats. You can also attach a cooler that can double as a seat for longer outings.

In Hawaii, spearfishing off a SUP is also popular. The SUP allows you to paddle out to harder-to-reach fishing spots and anchor the board while you dive for fish. The board provides a place to rest and to store and transport your catch.

Paddling with a Dog

Before attempting to paddle with a dog, make sure they're comfortable around water first:

>> Build confidence by starting slowly with short, light sessions close to shore.

>> Fit your dog with a floatation device that has a good fit for their size and a sturdy handle on the back that will help you lift them back onto the board if they fall in.

>> Slowly introduce the dog to the board, first on land and then with the board half on land and half in the water.

>> Reward them for good behavior with praise or treats and consider bringing a favorite toy on the board to keep them entertained.

Taking a special SUP dog lesson can be helpful for both you and your pet.

WARNING

When paddling with a dog, be ready for sudden movements. If you're paddling with a big dog and they suddenly move around on the board, expect that to challenge your balance.

TIP

Some dogs like to walk around on the board, although more timid dogs are usually most comfortable between your feet or, as they get more comfortable, they like to stand on the nose of the board. A traction pad that covers the full deck all the way to the nose is ideal as a board with no pad on the nose will be too slippery for your dog to stand on.

The annual Duke's OceanFest in Waikiki features a SurFur competition. Figure 22-2 shows Nick Freeman competing with SUPdog Phoenix.

FIGURE 22-2:
Nick Freeman with Phoenix.

Photo by Joseph Esser

Whitewater SUP

One of my most memorable experiences was paddling through the Grand Canyon on a SUP with the support of a group. Navigating fast-moving currents, rapids, and eddies is an exciting challenge that requires a different paddling skill set than traditional flat-water paddling or SUP surfing does. It's similar to whitewater kayaking, with the added challenge of maintaining balance while standing up and using a single-blade paddle.

When you combine the speed of the flowing river with your paddle speed, you can cover long distances. Going down a river is similar to doing SUP downwinders in that you usually meet your paddling partner(s) at the end point, leave a car at the take out, and then drive another car to the start. This approach involves a bit more planning and logistics, but you're rewarded with an exciting way to experience rivers and fast-moving water.

Boards designed for whitewater SUP are typically shorter, wide, and stable but also more maneuverable. They need to be more durable to withstand impacts with rocks and other obstacles, which are often impossible to avoid in rapids. Inflatable boards (see Figure 22-3) are well suited for whitewater paddling because they can bounce off rocks without sustaining major damage. Head to Chapter 3 for details on inflatable boards.

WARNING

A helmet, a personal floatation device, footwear, kneepads, and a waist leash with a quick release designed for whitewater are crucial pieces of safety gear because whitewater SUP carries the risk of bumping into rocks and obstacles. And if your leash gets caught on something (like a submerged branch) in a fast-moving current, reaching out to remove a regular surf leash from your ankle can be impossible. Chapter 5 has more on safety equipment basics.

TIP

Educate yourself about the risks involved before embarking on this extreme discipline. I highly recommend taking a class or lesson from an experienced whitewater paddler and starting slowly on easy river rapids to get used to the dynamics of whitewater because it's very different from ocean waves.

Daniel Gonzalez/Stocksy/Adobe Stock Photos

SUP Foiling

SUP foiling is one of the most exhilarating and challenging variations of the sport and has experienced rapid growth. *SUP foiling* involves attaching a *hydrofoil* (underwater fin) to the bottom of the board. The foil is built much like a small airplane, with a front wing that creates lift, a fuselage, and a tail wing that provides stability. A rod (called mast) connects the foil to your board. After you, the paddler, reach a certain speed, the foil creates enough lift to raise you and your board completely out of the water, allowing you to smoothly glide above the water surface with very little drag.

WARNING

Foiling requires advanced balance and paddle skills, so it's best suited for experienced paddlers. The sensation of flying over the water without the board touching the water is incredible — and very unnerving at first. Controlling the foil by using subtle shifts in weight placement is a completely new skill set, and the difficulty and risk involved is part of what makes the experience so rewarding.

SUP foiling commonly uses wave energy for propulsion, either by surfing breaking waves or by going downwind and riding open water wind swells. You *can* get up on foil in flat water by using paddle power and "pumping" the foil, but it's very challenging. SUP foiling boards are specifically designed for the conditions — typically long and narrow boards for downwind SUP foiling and shorter, wider ones for SUP foiling in breaking waves.

REMEMBER

SUP foiling is still a relatively new sport, and the equipment is evolving rapidly. Learning to foil is risky because you can fall on the winged blade beneath the board if your balance is slightly off, so I highly recommend taking lessons. Foil lessons usually involve getting a feel for the foil by using an *efoil* (a foil with an electric motor) or by towing behind a boat or personal watercraft — think Jet Ski — before using a paddle to catch waves.

SUP Rescue

The high vantage point, maneuverability, and paddling speed make SUPs a great rescue tool for lifeguards. In fact, open-water swimming events often use lifeguards on SUPs to provide water safety. In the following sections, I highlight a couple of SUP rescue methods.

REMEMBER

Practice rescue skills before you need them; it may help you save someone's life! By working on SUP rescue techniques or taking a course, you gain confidence that allows you to remain calm during an emergency. In rescue scenarios, quick decision making, strong paddling skills, and the ability to remain calm under pressure are critical. Being prepared to help in a real-life emergency makes all the difference if you ever need to use these skills.

Flip rescue

If a swimmer or paddler in distress is unconscious or too weak to get on a board, the *flip rescue* is the best way to get them onto your board and paddle them to safety:

1. **Flip the board upside down and get the victim's arms over the bottom of the board with their armpits over the board's rail.**

2. **From this position, use your body weight to pull on the victim's arms as shown in Figure 22-4 and flip the board over by putting your weight on the opposite rail.**

   This movement flips the board right side up with the victim ending up on the top of the board.

3. **Rotate the victim if necessary and place yourself behind them to paddle them to safety in a prone position.**

FIGURE 22-4: Performing a flip rescue.

For additional tips for flip rescues, check out this YouTube video I made: www.youtube.com/watch?v=Sud_r-zg8RU.

Towing

If another paddler is unable to get back to land on their own, towing them to safety is the best rescue option. To *tow* another board, your best bet is to attach a line to the nose of the board to be towed and to the tail of your board. If a line isn't available, and the board to be towed has no attachment point close to the nose, you can use your leash. Ask the person to be towed to lay prone on their board and then to hold your leash as close to the nose of their board as possible while you tow them. Don't use this method in strong winds as removing your own leash could result in losing both boards.

SUP Jousting

SUP jousting is a modern twist on medieval jousting. Rules can vary, but this activity usually involves two paddlers trying to knock each other off their boards by using the heavily padded end of a paddle. The padding usually includes pool noodles, foam pads, and tape. Some contests have elimination rounds, and the last person standing wins the jousting tournament.

TIP

For safety, a helmet, leash, and a life jacket are recommended.

SUP Team-Building Exercises

When paddling with a larger group, team-building exercises where the group splits up into smaller teams that compete with each other are often fun. They encourage teamwork, communication, and a healthy dose of competition in a fun environment.

Here are a few team building exercise ideas:

» **Treasure hunt:** The teams receive clues that help them find hidden objects along the course.

» **Obstacle course:** Teams navigate an obstacle course that can include different activities on the water and on land. Each team member has to complete a given task, solve a riddle, or pick up an object to bring to the finish line. All team members must finish together.

» **Relay race:** Each member of the team must paddle a short course (around a buoy and back), passing the board to the next team member, until the whole team completes the course.

SUP Drills

If you're coaching beginner paddlers, practicing technique elements by using drills that exaggerate the movements can be helpful.

For some ideas for drills that you can use while stranding in knee-deep water, check out this YouTube video I made that shows drills for getting a good catch, feathering the blade, and twisting the torso to propel yourself forward: youtu.be/okIPrX jAJe4?si=qTzQqQBxg1BvDGRM

As your skills improve, there are many ways to enjoy stand up paddleboarding, so keep it fun and interesting by trying some of the many exciting disciplines. Whether you feel like going on a long adventure tour, taking your board on a fishing expedition, participating in a calming SUP yoga class, practicing rescue techniques, or getting into the adrenaline-pumping challenges of whitewater SUP or SUP foiling, there are many ways to enjoy this great sport.

Chapter 23

School Smarts: Ten Resources for Learning More

SUP skills classes, retreats, and instructor certification courses are offered in many locations around the world, and lots of resources are also available online. In this chapter I provide a number of different resources for these options so you can continue your path of SUP growth. If you're interested in teaching others to stand up paddleboard, you can sign up for an instructor certification course through one of the organizations listed.

Beginner Lessons

You can find countless beginner SUP lessons available at every popular SUP destination through an online search.

The quality of beginner lessons varies widely and can depend on both the school and the instructor. Before signing up for a beginner lesson, find out

>> **Whether the instructors are certified by one of the associations I highlight in this chapter.**

>> **What the lesson includes.** Some "lessons" are really just rentals with a few questionable tips thrown in before the "instructor" sends you out on the water without any further help. On the other end of the spectrum are instructors who give invaluable hands-on instructions and tips tailored to help you improve quickly.

>> **What the online reviews have to say.**

I highly recommend the type of lesson with hand-on instruction. It's well worth the investment because it helps you avoid common issues early on before they become (bad) habits and accelerates your learning curve.

Advanced Classes

Many of the SUP schools that offer beginner classes (see the preceding section) also offer more advanced skills classes that can help you progress further. These classes are good opportunities to connect with others interested in the same development you are. Depending on the skills you want to pursue, you can take classes that focus on paddle technique, racing, downwinders, SUP surfing, whitewater, yoga, fitness, and more.

You can also sign up for longer advanced retreats held in destination locations, such as these:

>> The Blue Zone SUP Surf retreat in Nosara, Costa Rica (bluezonesup.com/).

>> The Kalama Kamps in Fiji (kalamakamp.com/).

>> A host of SUP yoga retreats offered by companies all over the world. (Check out www.bookyogaretreats.com/all/c/sup-yoga-retreats for an extensive list of locations.)

Training Groups

Meeting with other padders to train on a regular basis is an excellent way to improve your skills and fitness. My friend Jeff Chang and I ran a weekly SUP training group that met every Wednesday for over 15 years. We stopped during the COVID-19 pandemic shutdowns and (as of this writing) haven't started it back up again, but other groups of paddlers meet on a regular basis to paddle together. Find out about groups in your area though your local SUP retailer, Facebook groups, Meetup groups, and so on. Or start your own group!

Resources for Becoming a Certified SUP Instructor

If you are interested in becoming a certified SUP instructor yourself, here is list of five associations that offer instructor training classes:

Professional Stand Up Paddle Association (PSUPA)

The PSUPA website (www.psupa.com) has a list of certified SUP coaches that offer lessons as well as a directory of instructor certification courses offered by instructor trainers in North America and in Hawaii.

REMEMBER

Successful completion of the Flatwater Level 1 course is required prior to taking other certification courses, which include the following:

>> SUP yoga

>> River SUP

>> SUP surfing

>> Downwind SUP

>> Camp SUP

>> SUP Pilates and fitness certifications

World Paddle Association (WPA)

The WPA (www.worldpaddleassociation.com) provides several instructor levels based on each instructor's credentials and the needs within the stand up paddleboarding community. The levels offered are

>> SUP trained specialist (online exam only).

>> Class I (certified to teach lessons).

>> Class I Trainer (certified to teach a Class I course).

>> Class II (attend a class or online exam).

>> Class II Trainer (certified to teach Class I and Class II courses).

>> Class III (certified for flat water, open ocean, and wave surfing).

>> Master Class I.

American Canoe Association (ACA)

The ACA (www.americancanoe.org) offers SUP skill courses as well as instructor certifications for the following disciplines:

>> Flat Water SUP

>> River/Whitewater SUP

>> Surf SUP

>> Coastal SUP

International Surfing Association (ISA)

The International Olympic Committee (IOC) has recognized the ISA (www.isasurf.org) as the governing authority for the sport of SUP. You can read more about that in Chapter 16.

ISA coaching and instructor courses for SUP include these:

>> Flat Water SUP

>> Surf SUP

>> Open Water SUP

TECHNICAL STUFF

The ISA also offers courses for judging surf events, adaptive surfing, and water safety.

Paddle Fit

Paddle Fit (www.paddlefitpro.com) has a series of SUP instructional videos available on its website. It also offers various levels of instructor certification courses as well as coaching.

YouTube Channels

You can easily waste time going down rabbit holes on YouTube, but plenty of good information is available. The following list highlights some of my favorite channels, all with good SUP instructional videos, product reviews, tips, and interviews:

>> @blueplanetsurf: My business posts a new video every Saturday, including technique demonstrations, interviews, SUP gear reviews, foiling overviews, and looks at other watersports.

» **@SUPboardermag:** This channel offers lots of quality instructional videos and reviews. (**Note:** It's based in the United Kingdom.)

» **@totalSUP:** Here you can find news, interviews, and instructional videos.

» **@ethanhuffsup:** Check out this channel for easy-to-follow instructional videos.

» **@supboardguide:** Go here for good instructions and reviews of inflatable SUPs.

» **@standuppaddlingTV:** This channel has a good collection of instructional videos.

Other Online Resources

You can find countless resources available online, and separating marketing hype from useful information is often difficult. For the latest news and information on SUP, here are some of my favorite groups, forums, and websites:

» **Reddit/SUP** (www.reddit.com/r/Sup/): A big community with lots of iSUP enthusiasts posting regularly; a good place to post questions.

» **SUP Surfing Facebook Group** (www.facebook.com/groups/446598407248720/): A big group with regular updates and good information on SUP surfing.

» **Seabreeze.com.au** (https://www.seabreeze.com.au/forums/Stand-Up-Paddle/SUP): Australian forum with a global audience.

» **Standupzone.com** (www.standupzone.com/forum/): Formerly the most-active forum for SUP but has lost some momentum.

» **Swaylocks.com** (swaylocks.com/): Good forum for board building and repairs.

>> **Boardlady.com (boardlady.com/):** Great resource for complex epoxy board repairs.

>> **SUPracer.com (supracer.com/):** Insightful race news by SUP race enthusiast Chris Parker.

>> **Paddlemonster.com (paddlemonster.com/):** Great resource for race technique and training from champion SUP racer Larry Cain and buy and sell listings, mostly on the U.S. East Coast.

>> **Allpaddling.com (www.allpaddling.com/):** Excellent paddle-specific training plans and custom race plans from Australian Mick Di Betta. Mick is the winner of the first Molokai to Oahu Works Championship Paddleboard race held in 1997. He has trained countless champions and even in his sixties, is still a fierce competitor.

>> **Paddling.net (paddling.com/):** Good listing of available gear with reviews.

Appendix

SUP Lingo For Dummies

SUP TYPES

All-round (or cruiser): Versatile board shape for cruising and small waves

Downwind race board: Designed for catching open ocean swells

iSUP: Inflatable boards that are easy to transport and store

Foil SUP: Designed to work with a foil mounted under the board

Race board: Long and narrow displacement shape optimized for speed

River SUP: Maneuverable and stable board designed for whitewater

Surf SUP: Shorter board with curvy outline designed to excel in the waves

Touring SUP: Longer displacement-type shape with many attachment points

Wing SUP: Board with a sail attachment point that allows it to be used as a windsurf board

Yoga SUP: Wide and stable board designed for practicing yoga poses

HARDBOARD CONSTRUCTION

Carbon fiber: Stronger and stiffer than fiberglass but not as resilient

Blank: The foam core inside the board; can be shaped by hand, by a computer shaping machine, or molded

Epoxy resin: Two-part resin used to laminate most SUP boards

EPS (expanded polystyrene): Lightweight foam blank most commonly used for SUPs

EVA (ethylene vinyl acetate): Closed-cell (will not absorb water) soft foam used for deck pads

Fiberglass: Fabric-like woven sheets of thin glass threads, available in different weights

High density foam: Closed-cell (will not absorb water) foam (usually PVC) used as a thin layer in sandwich construction and around inserts to strengthen the weaker EPS foam core

Innegra: Highly resilient weave but difficult to sand

Kevlar: Another highly resilient weave that's difficult to sand

Laminating: The process of saturating flexible layers of woven materials with liquid resin that cures into a hard, solid surface

Polyester resin: Legacy resin used for surfboard construction; should not be used to repair epoxy boards

Sandwich construction: Layering different materials to create a thicker, stronger outer shell using a mold or vacuum bagging process

UV curing resin: Resin that cures when exposed to UV light

Wood veneer: Thin layer of wood or bamboo used between layers of fiberglass to strengthen the outer shell

ISUP CONSTRUCTION

Double-layer: Boards covered with a second layer of PVC for more durability and stiffness

Dropstitch: Thousands of internal threads that keep the top and bottom layers of a board flat and control the thickness of the board; dense, woven, heat-fused dropstitch material is the best technology as of this writing

Fusion: Process of bonding the layers (laminating) with heat and pressure; lighter, stronger, stiffer, more durable than glued construction

Recommended PSI: Amount of air pressure (in pounds per square inch) a board can handle; maximum recommended pressure is usually between 15 and 20 psi.

Sidewall construction: Makeup of the rails; plays a critical role in quality and longevity

Single-skin: Dropstitch material covered with a single layer of PVC; lightweight and inexpensive but more flexible and less durable than double-layer construction

Stringers: A variety of stiffening materials designed to reduce flex and bounce

TRACTION

Arch bar: Bump in the center of the tail pad under the arch of the foot that provides tactile foot placement feedback and traction

Deck pad: EVA foam pad that provides a grippy, comfortable surface

Tail kick: Raised bump at end of the tail pad for critical maneuvers; provides leverage and keeps the foot from sliding off the back of the board

Tail pad: Placed over the fins of surf SUPs to provide back-foot traction for maneuvers

Wax mat: Thinner, lighter traction without padding

BOARD ATTRIBUTES

Action camera mount: Some boards have a recessed insert on the nose that allows you to mount an action camera attachment

Bottom: The board side facing the water

Boxy/full rails: Thick rails with more volume; make the board more stable and forgiving

Deck: The top of the board

Dimensions/specs: The length, width, thickness (usually measured in feet and inches) and volume (in liters) of a board; may also include the weight

Glide: How well a board moves through the water

Leash: Safety strap that attaches you to the board

Leash plug: Plug on the tail of the board to attach a leash

Nose: The front end of the board

Pin tail: Tail that comes to a sharp point; used for big waves and advanced conditions

Rails: The sides of the board

Rail tape: Protective tape applied to the rails of the board to protect it from paddle strikes and scratches when you set the board down on the rails

Round tail: Hybrid between a squash tail and pin tail

Squash tail: Square tail shape with rounded corners; versatile, most common

Swallow tail: Tail shape with two tips; used on surf SUPs

Tail: The back end of the board

Tapered rails: Thinned-out rail shape that bites into the wave better; good for performance surfing and critical conditions but not as stable as full rails

Vent plug: Allows air pressure between the foam core and the outside to neutralize; most have a self-venting membrane that allows air (but not water) to pass through

Volume: The amount of floatation or buoyancy a board has; measured in liters

DECK/HULL TYPES

Displacement hull: A rounded bottom shape and curvy rails designed to pierce through the water and direct the water flow around the hull; creates less drag at normal paddle speeds than a planing hull

Domed deck: A rounded deck shape often seen on surfboards; not as comfortable to stand on as a flat deck

Dugout: A deeply recessed standing area used on race boards to lower the center of gravity to improve balancing of narrow boards

Planing hull: A flat bottom board with sharp rails in the back that allows the board to create lift and slide over the water (plane) at higher speeds, reducing the wetted area

Recessed deck: A deck where the standing area is slightly concave and recessed

FINS FINS

Base: Measurement from lowest front point to the rearmost point of the fin

Depth: Length of fin; the exposed height of the fin as measured from bottom of board to the tip of the fin

Fin box(es): The area or areas on the bottom of the board that allow fins to be installed and removed

Fin setup: The arrangement and number of fins on a board, which can affect performance and handling

Rake: Measurement of how far behind the trailing edge of the base the tip of the fin extends

Single fin: One larger center fin; tracks well, has the least drag, and is the most versatile

Skeg: Another name for fins

U.S. center fin box: Standard-size center fin box that can accommodate a wide variety of fins

FIN SETUPS FOR SUP SURFING

2+1: A three-fin setup with a larger center fin and two smaller side fins

Quad fins: Uses four side fin boxes consisting of front and rear quad fins; provides good speed and hold on faster waves

Thruster: Using three fins that are close to equal in size, one in the center fin box and two in the forward side fin boxes; provides good drive, stability, and control

PADDLE ATTRIBUTES

Blade: The flat, wide end of the paddle that grabs the water

Blade edge: The thin outer perimeter edge of the paddle blade

Blade size: Usually measured in square inches of surface area

Flutter: The tendency of the blade to wander from side to side during the power phase

Dihedral: The raised spine shape on the face of the blade to direct water flow and minimize flutter

Handle: The top end of the paddle that the upper hand grips and pushes down on

Neck: The transition between the shaft and the blade

Paddle guard: Protective material applied to the paddle edge to protect both the blade edge and the rails of the board from getting damaged if the paddle hits the rails

Power face: The side of the blade that compresses against the water

Shaft: The long, straight round or oval portion of the paddle between the handle and the blade

Tapered shaft: A paddle shaft that tapers from a thicker diameter to a thinner diameter

PADDLE TECHNIQUE TERMINOLOGY

Active stance: A slightly bent knee posture to improve balance and control

Catch: The phase of the paddle stroke where the blade enters the water

Feathering: Rotating the power face of the blade outward during the release and recovery phases

Forward stroke: Stroke that provides maximum forward propulsion

Power phase: Where power is applied to the stroke to propel the board forward past the planted blade

Reach: The forwardmost part of the stroke where the blade enters the water

Recovery: The part of the stroke where you bring the paddle back forward into the reach position

Release: The phase of the stroke where the paddle blade exits the water

Reverse steering stroke: A reverse paddle stroke used to slow down or turn the board

Steering stroke: A sweeping paddle stroke to turn the board

Stroke rate: The cadence or number of strokes per minute

Strokes per side: Number of strokes taken on one side of the board before switching to the other side

Tracking: How well a board goes in a straight line without yawing

Yaw: The tendency of the board to turn while you're paddling on one side

SUP SURFING TERMINOLOGY:

Backside: Position where your back is facing the wave

Barrel: The hollow opening inside of a clean, fast breaking wave

Bottom turn: Turning from the trough of the wave back toward the steep part of the wave face by digging the rails into a carving turn

Bump: Unbroken swells in deeper, open water; can be wind swells (generated by local wind) or ground swells (generated elsewhere)

Cutback: Turning from the shoulder of the wave back toward the powerful pocket of the wave

Cross stepping: A smooth and stylish way to move up and down the board with feet and legs crossing over each other (rather than shuffling the feet)

Dropping in: Catching a wave in front of a surfer with priority (that is, the surfer closest to the wave peak); considered poor etiquette

Dynamic lift: The hydrodynamic lift generated by the board moving over the water surface (as opposed to static lift generated by the buoyancy of the board)

Face: The steep, sloping side of the wave that stands up before breaking

Floater: Move that involves riding along the top of a crashing lip before coming back down over the back of the breaking wave

Frontside: Position where your chest is facing the wave

Goofy foot: Surf stance with the right foot forward and left foot back

Grom: A young surfer

Hollow: Steep, powerful, barreling waves

Hanging ten: Surfing with both feet on the front of the board and all ten toes hanging off the nose of the board (also see nose riding)

Impact zone: The most powerful area of the surf zone where the waves peak and break

Kook: Beginner or someone who is unaware of their surroundings

Left hander: A wave that breaks toward the left from the surfer's vantage point

Lip: The tip of the wave that throws out over the bottom of the wave as it slows down over shallow bottom contours

Mushy: Describes soft and weaker-breaking waves that don't get very steep and crumbles (gently rolling white water) from the top; ideal for beginners

Neutral stance: Feet parallel to the board, toes pointing forward

Nose riding: Surfing on a wave with both feet close to the nose of the board

Off the lip: A critical maneuver where a surfer turns sharply at or near the breaking lip

Offshore: A wind that blows toward the ocean; creates cleaner waves

Onshore: A wind that blows toward the shore; creates mushy conditions

Parallel stance: Standing on the board with feet close to the rails and toes pointed forward

Peak: The tallest crest of the wave where the wave starts to break

Pearling: When the nose of the board gets pushed underwater as the wave lifts up the tail when catching a wave

Planing: (see also dynamic lift and wetted surface) When the board slides over the water surface and the weight is supported by hydrodynamic lift rather than volume/buoyancy

Pocket: The most powerful and critical part of a wave, where the face is steepest; closest to the breaking lip

Quiver: An assortment of boards designed for various conditions

Regular foot: Surf stance with left foot forward, right foot back

Right hander: A wave that breaks toward the right from the surfer's vantage point

Set: A group of larger waves (usually three to ten) followed by smaller waves

Shoulder: The sloping side of the face away from the breaking wave

Snaking: Paddling around another surfer to give yourself priority; considered poor etiquette

Staggered stance: Feet are staggered with one foot farther forward and one farther back for more front-to-back stability

Surf stance: Feet sideways along the center line of the board, like on a skateboard

Swing weight: Board weight further away from the center of rotation (towards the nose of the board). In essence, shorter, lighter boards have less swing weight which and require less effort to change direction.

Takeoff: The moment the board speeds up and slides down the face of the wave

Trough: The lowest, bottom part of the wave

Wave hog: Someone catching all the best waves without regard to other surfers

Wetted surface: the amount of board touching the water while planing over the water surface. The faster the board is moving, the less wetted surface is needed to support the weight.

Whitewater: The foaming wave that rolls toward shore after the wave face falls in on itself

Index

A

ACA (American Canoe Association), 210, 264

access rules, 86

action camera mount, 271

active recovery activities, 244

active stance, 274

adjustable paddle, 47, 48, 49–50

adventure racing, 178

African dugout canoe, 12

Ah Choy, John ("Pops"), 14

all-around boards, 37–38, 269

Allpaddling, 267

aluminum paddle, 48

American Canoe Association (ACA), 210, 264

anaerobic, 126

ankle cuffs, 53, 54, 92, 99

apparel, dressing for success, 63–68

apps
    Elite HRV app, 246
    fitness apps, 246
    Garmin Connect app, 246

arch bar, 271

attachment points, 24

automated distress signals, 59

B

backside, 275

balance
    re-boarding and regaining of, 99–100
    as strengthening and toning core, 155

balance domes, 75–76

balance tips, 96–97

balance training, 74–76, 77, 129, 156–157, 247

barrel, 275

barreling waves, 141

base, 273

Battle of the Paddle (Dana Point), 15–16, 175

beach boys, 12

beginner board/starter board, 32, 42

beginner lessons, 261–262

big wave guns, 39–40

big-box stores, for board purchase, 226

blade (of paddle), 44–45, 274

blade angle, perfecting yours, 234

blade edge, 274

blank, 269

Blue Planet Adventure Company, 91, 209

Blue Planet Kai Zen V3, 49

Blue Planet Surf, 15, 74, 164, 265

Blue Zone SUP Surf retreat (Nosara, Costa Rica), 262

board bag, 192, 210–211

board cover, 192, 193

board handling blunders
    coming in hot: trying to dismount too quickly/ from standing, 105–106
    not balancing weight at center of board, 104–105
    not keeping goal in mind, 107

not lifting up board correctly at end of day, 106

not paddling upwind first, 107

Boardlady, 267

boards
    accepting trade-offs of, 147
    all-around boards, 37, 37–38
    beginner board/starter board, 32, 42
    bells and whistles for, 26
    carrying, 93
    cheap boards, 34–35
    custom boards, 36
    design philosophies of, 27
    dimensions of, 20–21
    finding right one for you, 41–42
    fishing boards, 252
    giant boards, 161
    groveler SUP surf boards, 40
    hard boards. See hard boards
    high performance SUP surf boards, 40
    how water gets into, 194
    inflatable as compared to hard, 32
    inflatable boards (iSUPs). See inflatable boards (iSUPs)
    keeping yours on straight and narrow, 97–99
    kinds of matched with appropriate conditions, 223
    length of, 16
    lifting up correctly at end of day, 106

boards *(continued)*

maintenance of, 182–187

MegaSUP boards, 161

narrow boards, 20, 174, 256

as needing to be trimmed well, 160

parts of, 22–25

putting in water, 93

questions to ask before buying, 219–228

race boards, 20, 25, 27, 28, 38–39, 119, 223, 250

renting of, 211–212

rocker boards, 76

roller boards, 75, 76

securing to vehicle, 82–85

shapes of, 27

sharing of, 219

steering clear of handling blunders, 104–107

SUP surfing boards, 23, 28, 37, 39–40

SUPsquatch boards, 161

tippy board, 75

touring boards, 27, 37, 38, 223, 250

trying before you buy, 41

types of, 37–40

weight and construction as mattering, 34–36

width of, 20

body position, for SUP, 97

Bombers (floating sunglasses), 69

Bono Tidal Bore, Indonesia, 206

booties, 64, 66, 139

bottom, 271

bottom turns, 145–146, 275

Boundary Waters Canoe Area (Minnesota), 207

box breathing, 78

boxy/full rails, 271

Bradley, Todd, 15

Bradner, Hugh, 65

breathing exercises, 77, 78–79, 130, 235, 245

breathing meditation, 78

buddy system, 54, 55, 60, 87–88

budget, as balanced with performance, regarding board purchase, 225

Buffalo Big Board Surfing Classic (Makaha), 15, 161

bumps (wind waves), 153, 275

buoyant vests (Type II PFD), 56, 57

buying paddleboard, questions to ask yourself beforehand, 219–228

C

C4 Waterman, 15

caballitos de totora (reed horses), 10

Cain, Larry, 174

calories, shedding of, 153–154

cam buckle straps, 82

Canoe Single, 174

canter (of paddle), 45

Cape Town (South Africa), as windy place for SUP downwinders, 204

carbon fiber, 269

carbon paddles, 48

cardiovascular training/workouts, 77, 130, 152–153

CAS (Court of Arbitration for Sport), 169

casual paddling, as possible goal/ambition, 224

catch (stroke phase), 112, 229–230, 274

catch, power phase, exit, recovery (CPER), as stroke phases, 112–116

caught inside (in surfing), 138

cellphones (communication device), 58

certifications (instructor training), 209–210, 261, 263

Chang, Jeff, 15, 202

channel 16 (international channel for distress calls), 59

charity events, 166

Cheat Sheet, 5

Chiama (Peru), riding longest waves in world, 205

choppy water, board recommendation for, 223

Chun, Malama, 14

classes, 261–265

closure coming undone (leash failure), 54

CO_2 cartridge, 56, 57

coiled leashes, 52, 53

cold plunge, 129

color (of board), deciding if that matters, 227–228

Colorado River, 208

Columbia River Gorge (Oregon), as windy place for SUP downwinders, 203

common sense, use of, 56

communication devices, 55, 58–59

competition, getting into competitive spirit, 161–162

conditions for paddling, considering what conditions you'll be paddling in most often, 222–223

consideration of others, 85–88

contrast therapy, 129, 245

core, of hard board, 188–189

racing *(continued)*

Molokai to Oahu (M2O) Paddleboard World Championships. *See* Molokai to Oahu (M2O) Paddleboard World Championships

in Olympics, 169–170

as outgrowth of SUP, 15

as possible goal/ambition, 224

race-day strategies, 131–132

relay racing, 164

SUP racing, 15, 16, 124, 163–164, 172–179

technical racing, 16, 173–175

training program for, 125–128

racing events, 133

rack pads, 82

rail saver, 53, 92

rail tape, 272

rails

beefed-up rails, 183–184

defined, 272

described, 22–23

hard rails, 22

on planing hulls, 28

sharp rails, 28, 39

soft rails, 22–23

tips for keeping them in good shape, 193

Rainbow Sandals, 15

Rainer, Skyla, 146

rake, 273

reach, 275

re-boarding, 99–100

recessed deck, 273

recommended PSI, 271

recovery (stroke phase), 115–116, 231, 275

recovery, rest and, importance of, 127–128

Reddit/SUP, 266

"reef safe" sunscreens, 69

reef walkers, 66

reentry (aka off the lip) (in surfing), 147

reflexes, SUP as helping develop, 157–158

regular foot (in surfing), 140, 277

relay racing, 164

releasing, 28, 275

repair kit, 186, 187, 197

rescues, 256–257

resources, for learning more, 261–267

responsibilities

access rules, 86

etiquette, 85

knowing local access rules, 85

respecting local laws, 85, 86–87

rest and recovery, importance of, 244

retail stores (SUP-focused), 15

retreats, 261, 262

reverse J stroke, 117

reverse steering stroke, 275

reverse strokes, 98–99, 118

reverse sweep strokes, 98–99, 118, 119

rhythm, getting into, 234–235

riding down the line, 145

right of way, 87

river mouths, currents at, 73

river trips, 208

rivers, board recommendation for, 223, 269

rocker, 23

rocker boards, 76

rocker line, 40, 183–184, 188

roller boards, 75, 76

roof racks, 82

rookie mistakes, avoiding most common ones, 101–107

rotator cuff exercises, 129

round tail, 272

S

Sacramento River (California), 208

Saenz, Zane, 40

safety equipment. *See also* emergency equipment; *specific items*

importance of, 51

local laws about, 86

sandwich construction, 270

satellite communication devices, 59

sauna, 129

sea legs, finding yours, 19, 95, 96

Seabreeze, 266

secondhand, for board purchase, 226–227

self-rescue, 55

set, 277

Severn Bore, England, 206

shaft (of paddle), 45, 274

shaft angle, stacking shoulders to improve, 233–234

shaka ("hang loose"), 102

"a shaka over the head" (method for determining right paddle length), 46

sharp rails, 28, 39

shore break, 142

shortboard surfers, 136

shoulder impingement syndrome, 238

shoulder injuries, 238–239

shoulders

stacking of, 118, 233–234

of waves, 277

side fins, 26

About the Author

Robert Stehlik started his business, Blue Planet Surf, in 1993 as a business college project while a student at the University of Hawaii-Manoa. His mission statement? Helping people have more fun on the water! Blue Planet was one of the first businesses to distribute stand up paddleboards when the sport grew rapidly in the early 2000s, and Robert became heavily involved not only in sales and marketing but also in designing and manufacturing boards. To top it all off, he devoted his energies to teaching and coaching the sport as well as competing in as many competitions as possible.

Two advisors encouraged Robert to brand himself as the "SUP expert," which he took to heart by writing a blog, making instructional videos, recording interviews, doing podcasts, becoming a certified instructor trainer, attending trade shows, and competing as an athlete around the world.

Robert has competed in the Molokai to Oahu Paddleboard World Championships since 2009 and won the Men's SUP Solo Stock division in 2024 while writing this book.

Author's Acknowledgements

Even though I had no experience as an author, I jumped at the offer from Wiley Publishing to write Stand Up Paddleboarding For Dummies as an opportunity to share the joy of "walking on water" with a worldwide audience.

I've always thought it would be cool to author a book but had no idea how to even get started. Although I was excited about the project, I must admit that I really struggled to sit down and focus on writing the chapters, I couldn't have done it without the support I received.

A big thank you to the "For Dummies" team, without the structure, feedback, and support they provided, it would have been impossible for me to write this book.

I'm grateful to my wife Sharon for her unwavering support and positivity. Many thanks to Blue Planet cameraman Lucas Purcell for taking most of the instructional photos contained in this book.

As a SUP athlete, I am grateful to the founders of C4 Waterman (Dave Parmenter, Brian Keaulana, and Todd Bradley) for introducing me to the sport of SUP surfing and later downwind racing. In the early days of SUP, there was very little instructional content available, and they shared many helpful tips with me, some of which I still share today, including in this book.

Jeff Chang has played a big role in my life as a Stand Up Paddleboarder. Thank you, Jeff, for being my coach and training partner when I first started training for the Molokai Race. Jeff is humble and unassuming yet an incredible athlete and role model. Jeff and I coached a weekly training group on Oahu for over 10 years that has allowed us to hone our skills, stay in shape, and share our knowledge.

The regulars in the training group have kept me motivated and in shape over the years. Although we no longer meet every week, I'm fortunate to have a group of strong, stoked paddlers to train with and learn from, including Roland Graham, Jimmy Martindale, and others.

As a business owner, I must thank the amazing Blue Planet staff members for running the business while I'm out on the water having fun or traveling the world. I'm grateful to our loyal customers that support our small business and allow us to keep living the dream.

Being a member of the Entrepreneurs Organization has taught me to "work on the business, not in the business," and to keep a healthy balance between work and life. I always look forward to the monthly meetings with my EO forum group.

Publisher's Acknowledgments

Acquisitions Editor: Jennifer Yee

Senior Project Editor:
Paul Levesque

Copy Editor: Megan Knoll

Tech Reviewer: J. Tyler Landon

Production Editor:
Saikarthick Kumarasamy

Cover Images: © edb3_16/Getty Images, Courtesy of Robert Stehlik